GYŐZŐ BEZERÉDY

PÉCS

MECSEK-TOURIST
Baranya County Tourist Office
1986

Original Text supervised by
DR. LÁSZLÓ SZITA, LÁSZLÓ TISZAY

Translation:
SUSY SZÉCSI

Translation revised by
LEN SCOTT

Photographs by
KÁROLY CSONKA

Maps by
MRS. B. CSÁNYI

Arranged for printing by
PANORÁMA

ISBN 963 243 606 7

Printing office „Széchenyi" Győr 86. K—594
Director of printing office: Iván Nagy
Responsible editor: Magda Borsai
Technical Manager: Márton Orlai
Technical editor: Johanna Bede
Length: 7 in A/5 format printer's sheets +
3 maps and 32 pages of photographs

CONTENTS

TOWN AT THE FOOT OF THE MECSEK

"The first foundation of Pécs fades away into the shadows of ancient times. Its beautiful situation at the foot of the mountain, its numerous abundantly gushing wells, its luxuriously yielding area and its pleasant climate all make it believable, moreover certain, that it already existed before our era." This is how Mihály Haas, a reputed writer started his chronicle about our town in 1845, who was repeatedly fascinated by the magic of the land, the Mecsek, the vineyards and orchards, and the small town leaning on the mountain slope. From wherever a stranger arrives, he is greeted with a wonderful spectacle. The panorama is particularly enchanting from the direction of Siklós, the traveller arriving from Siklós will spontaneously exclaim at the first glance: "This would be the place for us, this is where we would like to build our home"—Haas wrote. Naturally, this was not the only reason why the town evolved here and in this manner. Its beautiful situation and the panorama mattered the least, the protective proximity of the Mecsek was much more important, together with the abundance and purity of the healthy karst waters, their usable rapid flow, and not least the important route which crossed the place from Byzantium to Regensburg. Man settled here in the hope of a secure life, at the meeting place of the mountains and the plain, on the fertile soil and under a favourable climate.

Up till now the Mecsek has retained its determinative significance. It remained a source of the town's riches. Most probably the Romans were the first settlers of the Pécs *vineyards*, in the Middle Ages wine coming from Pécs was considered one of the best in the whole country, and in Turkish times in addition to white wine, the red one was also acclimatized. The "kadarka" brought from the Skadar (Uskudar) soon

7

acquired great renown and the Turks not only traded with it, but drank a lot, although this was strongly forbidden by their religion.

Orchards also spread over the area. Janus Pannonius, the great Hungarian humanist poet, described the flourishing almond trees in a beautiful poem, and Evlia Tchelebi, the Turkish traveller and historian, mentioned the varied luxurious orchards: apricots and brambles, and then wrote: "Reliable old people explained that they made a list of 170 species of pears and this is true. My poor soul, when I was guest of the Bey in the neighbourhood of the Szigeti Gate, my host brought out all the types of pears to be found in his house and one day I ate 42 different pears, each was of a different flavour, with a sweetish piquant juice and pleasant scent." During the Turkish domination, the orchards of Pécs started to flourish. Cherry, apricot, peach, pear and plum trees could be found in every vineyard. Fig trees became acclimatized in the protected spots, and today they are still available, abundantly growing fruit under the protection of sun baked old houses and fences.

In 1845, Miksa Hölbling, a known writer and physician, wrote the following about the Pécs orchards: "Until now, 61 different noble species of apples were grown in the neighbourhood of Pécs... there are 66 species of pears around Pécs. Mostly apricots and plum trees prefer the Pécs region... there are 35 different types of apricots here..." Since then, the vineyards were damaged by phylloxera, the orchards by feverish building work, and the ancient grape vines and fig trees were effected by urbanisation, nevertheless, fruit and wine from Pécs are still household words. In old times, both were the source of the prosperity of the town. Merchants sought after them, it was worthwhile to travel from distant areas. Thus, the Mecsek had a decisive role in the life of the town. On its southern side, stretching from the Makár mountain to Szabolcs, a continuous and extensive strip of vineyards and orchards ensured a livelihood, moreover, prosperity for the population.

In the second half of the 18th century, coal was found and mining started with intensity from the

1840s and the first factories at Pécs were already relying on *coal*. From 1852, managed by the Danube Steam Shipping Company, coal from Pécs made the town known all over the monarchy. In the second half of the 20th century, mining of *uranium* started. This was the third major gift of the Mecsek.

The inhabitants of Pécs are fond of the Mecsek, and the guests visiting the town soon become fond of it. No wonder! It simply cannot be ignored. Which ever street of the town one takes a stroll through, a part of the Mecsek always appears in the background, sometimes from the blueish distance, on other occasions in an arms-length proximity. The streets of Pécs do not exist without the Mecsek. Jakab mountain, Makár mountain or the Tubes, then the Misina or Havi mountain, perhaps the Kálvária Hill appear from behind the old houses. The Mecsek is an inseparable part and component of the town.

One can safely say: the Mecsek is always the greatest everyday experience of the people of Pécs. Nobody can ignore it, even if they never climb it. Living anywhere in the town, the first glance in the morning will catch the mountain, if the sun shines one can see the Mecsek bathed in light, if there is a storm—green with anger, in bad weather—concealed by humidity and fog, or sparkling with white snow. And if one climbs the mountain, a glance from every rest spot and from every curve of the road—takes in the town. The Mecsek and Pécs are inseparable.

THE HISTORY OF PÉCS

FROM PRE-HISTORICAL TIMES UNTIL THE CONQUEST OF THE MAGYARS

Pécs is frequently mentioned as the "2,000-year-old town". In fact the town itself evolved much earlier, and man settled here for the first time many thousands of years ago. This is confirmed by the large number of finds. According to specialists, the area of the present-day town and its surroundings were first permanently populated in about the fifth millennium BC. According to the finds, the people of the so-called *linear pottery culture* lived here in the Neolithic Age. Finds from the *Neolithic* and *Bronze Age* were discovered in the area of the Makár mountain and Málom, and relics from the *Copper Age* were found on the southern slope of the Mecsek, in the neighbourhood of the Makár mountain, Rácváros. Vasas and Szabolcs, and also in the Ürögi Valley and Üszög. At the end of the Bronze Age, the *urn field people* settled at the Danube and the Dráva rivers, then were replaced by the people of the *Hallstatt culture,* who already knew iron. They arrived in the 8th century B.C., and occupied the mountains. They built extensive settlements protected by earthwork on the Mecsek and at Jakab mountain, where they built a centre of bronze and iron craft. This fortress-like site on the high plateau was a centre of trade for centuries. Most probably the people of the Hallstatt culture also built their centre on Jakab mountain.

The first peoples mentioned by written sources were the *Illyrians* and the *Pannons,* who were followed in the 6th and 5th centuries B.C. by the *Celts.* They constituted the ancient population, who were conquered by the *Romans* around the beginning of A.D. The first known name of Pécs was *Sopianae.* This town was set up approximately in the second century B.C. It was founded by the local inhabitants and the Pannons and Illyrians, who were immigrants from

the west. In 10 B.C., Sopianae became part of the
vast Roman Empire, one of the small towns of a distant province. A small town, but not insignificant. Its
significance was due to the junction of important roads
coming from even more distant areas. These roads
were important from the trade viewpoint, but primarily because of their strategic position. The difficult
struggles fought against the barbarians further increased the importance of the town. After 293 A.D. Sopianae became the centre of the civil administration
of the newly organised province of Valeria. This
launched the town on the road to considerable prosperity. Large construction work started, palaces, villas
and public buildings were erected. This was also the
period when *Christianity* spread in the area. During
the recent building work, numerous relics of that
period were found in the inner-city, around the Cathedral, including graves, painted and plain burial
vaults, and graveyard chapels.

In the late imperial period, the Roman Empire underwent grave crises. The militant peoples living
beyond the frontiers—called *barbarians* by the Romans
—weakened the defensive power of the Empire, with
continuous attacks. Due to their attacks, Sopianae also
started to decline. Its inhabitants fled to more secure
places, primarily to Italy and the Balkans. However,
the town did not become completely depopulated.
Many people lived through the difficult times, and
during the migration of the peoples banded together
with newly appearing peoples.

In fact, Roman superiority did not cease from one
day to another, but in a gradual manner. From 433 to
455, Pécs and its surroundings belonged to the *Hun
Empire*. Then between 455 and 470, it was taken over
by the *Eastern Goths*. From 470, the *East Roman
Empire* extended its rule over the area, then from
504 again the *Eastern Goths* gained the upper hand
over the former Sopianae and its neighbourhood. In
546, the *Longobards* replaced them: they were followed in 568 by the *Avars*. Avar rule lasted until 803,
and from then until the end of the century, the area
was ruled by the *Carolingian state*. In the Frank Empire, the town—which again started to flourish—was

given a new name: Quinque Basilicae. According to our knowledge, Archbishop Liupramm of Salzburg consecrated a church here, perhaps the one which laid the foundations for the present Cathedral. Most probably the population of the town was a mixture of all the peoples who set foot here during the great migration. Most of them were Avars. Perhaps they lived here in the largest grouping during the conquest, and merged with the Magyars.

We know very little and only generalities about the *conquest of the Magyars*. Without doubt, the Hungarians when occupying the area, found a settled population here, mostly Avars. According to the chronicler Anonymus, the Hungarians arrived here around 899, led by Ete and Bojta. Archeological relics from the era of the conquest found at Pécs are preserved by the archeological department of the Janus Pannonius Museum, and the more significant ones are on view at a permanent exhibition.

The history of Pécs had three major periods. The first was the history of Sopianae in the Roman age, the other two took place in the Middle Ages. Despite the fact that—as a consequence of the Turkish occupation—almost nothing survived intact from the Middle Ages, the fragments allow us to presume a very high standard urban life and flourishing culture. We know very little about the events of the medieval history of Pécs, in fact the gathering and processing of the medieval documentary material preserved in other archives only starts nowadays. However, archeological finds were discovered over the past 100 years, in such large numbers on the site of the town during building work and reconstructions, that in Romanesque Hungarian architecture and arts, we have been speaking about the Pécs School for a long time, knowing that it was in contact with the artistic life of period Europe and its effect radiated all over the Carpathian Basin.

The other major period was the renaissance, probably nourished by the university set up in 1367—for the first time in Hungary. This development was most certainly affected by Italy, which was not far away. Real prosperity was enhanced by the humanist Pécs bishops and priests (Janus Pannonius, Zsigmond Hampó, Zsigmond Ernuszt, György Szatmáry, and István Brodarics) who were able to create a humanist centre with centuries-long influence on this well established area, in the sphere of the attraction of Italy, and in an extremely dangerous period in the shadow of constant threats from Turkish attacks.

PÉCS IN THE MIDDLE AGES

When the organisation of the Hungarian state started, the significance of Pécs was temporarily pushed into the background. Baranyavár became the seat of the newly constructed county. Nevertheless, during his church organisational activity, King Stephen donated a central place for Pécs. In his *charter dated August 23, 1009* the King announced the foundation of the Pécs bishopric. Obviously the reason for his choice of Pécs was the almost 1,000 year old tradition of Christianity, it was a place inhabited by a considerable number of Christians and the century-old consecrated churches were still extant. According to some opinions, the graveyard chapel (cella trichora) built around the 4th century was used for several centuries. It is also probable that this was the seat of the bishopric already after 313, therefore, later a basilica was built, presumably on the site of the present Cathedral. We have very few data about the building of the first cathedral, however, it is known that the church was totally destroyed by fire in 1064. This was followed by grandiose construction work, which probably lasted until the first quarter of the 12th century. Its extant relics, carved stonework and statues still fascinate observers. This was not simply reconstruction after the fire, but the linking or extension of the ancient Christian, Slav and later architecture from the period of St. Stephen into an organic ensemble. Simultaneously, the building wes richly decorated with sculpture. Both the interior and external decor of the Cathedral, and the uniquely attractive folk altar, reflect the handiwork of Lombard, presumably Pavian masters. French influence is reflected

13

by the sculptures of the famous entrance to the crypt. Led by masters from abroad, a local school of sculpture developed, stone masons of this school carried out a significant part of the work. The fertile effect of the flourishing workshop can only be discovered on the other secular and ecclesiastic constructions in Pécs, and the recently discovered rich architectural sculpture finds allow us to make such conclusions.

The medieval history of Pécs—similarly to the other county and bishopric seats—may have been very rich, nevertheless, we know very little about it. It must have been an eminent place as an ecclesiastic centre. because it had very famous bishops in the Middle Ages. The first bishop was *Bonipert* of French origin, then from 1036 *Mór* (Saint Maurice). The foundation of the Order of St. Paul, the only order founded by a Hungarian, is linked with the name of Bishop *Bertalan* (Bartholomew), who lived in the 13th century. (The ruins of their first monastery are at the moment being reconstructed on Jakab mountain.) Nevertheless, the best known was Bishop John, who was nobody else but *Janus Pannonius,* the poet known all over Europe in his period. The line of humanist bishops was opened with *Zsigmond Hampó,* the founder of the first public library. *György Szatmáry*—in very hard times—built a renaissance palace and summer resort, and ordered a wonderful carved altar (Szatmáry pastoforium, a tabernacle). *Fülöp Móré,* the last bishop of pre-Mohács times, perished on the battlefield.

In the Middle Ages, Pécs was one of the significant cultural centres of Hungary. Bishop Mór wrote his main work, the Legend of St. Benedict in Latin at Pécs after 1064. One of our finest codex relics is the Pécs Codex and the incunabulum Pécs Missale made in Venice in 1499 for an order from Pécs. The great poet Janus Pannonius and Bishop Hampó both possessed famous libraries. The most important manifestation of Hungarian medieval intellectual life was the foundation of the first Hungarian university in 1367. Unfortunately we know very little about the Pécs university, the names of its teachers and students were washed away by time, and we do not even know the

14

site of the university, it may have been situated somewhere around the present István square.

The Cathedral was an outstanding creation of medieval local architecture, but the St. Bertalan Church may also have been a significant building. The Palace of Bishop Szatmáry and his summer resort at Tettye were fine examples of *renaissance* architecture.

DURING TURKISH OCCUPATION

This flourishing cultural life at Pécs was destroyed by the Turks in the mid-16th century. After losing the battle at Mohács, the inhabitants of Pécs suffered difficult tribulations. There was no one to curb the ravages of the foraying Turkish troops. Those who would have been suitable, died on the battlefield of Mohács, others fled or utilizing the confused situation, rivalled the Turks in looting. Baranya County and the town of Pécs remained completely defenceless. The chaos was made worse by the dual king election. The forces were further reduced, because the Hungarian population of Pécs supported King John, and the German inhabitants supported Ferdinand. In 1528, Ferdinand freed the town from the burden of taxation for 12 years and in compensation asked the burghers to strengthen the walls and make the town defendable. However, this bid not take place and no help came. Thus, in 1543 the Turks occupied the town without any resistance.

Anyway resistance would have been in vain. The low walls were in such a poor condition that they were not suitable for defence. An eye witness, the historian Istvánffy wrote the following about this: " ... neither nature nor craft defends the town. A very high mountain, the Mececus (Mecsek) towers behind it, from where it is very easy to shoot with guns. The walls and the towers were built according to the old fashion, but they stood half in ruins ..."

Simultaneously with the occupation of Pécs, almost the whole of Baranya County was lost. Until 1566, Pécs belonged to the Mohács, after 1566 to the Sziget-vár military district (Sanjak). In 1600 (after the occupation of Kanizsa), Pécs became a seat of the Sanjak Bey.

During the 143 years of Turkish rule, Pécs acquired an Oriental character. The Hungarian population was slowly pushed out from the wall protected town, and settled around the All Saints Church, south of the Tettye. The downtown houses were occupied by Turks, Greek merchants, Bosnians and marauders of different nationalities (Marauders street)—primarily Serbians—and changed the profile of the town to suit their own taste. Oriental bazaars appeared on the squares (Main square) and on the main streets with the small workshops of the craftsmen. The colourful whirlpool of Oriental life took place in the houses "inherited" from the Middle Ages, and in wooden stands set up in the streets and squares. The military town of Pécs became a town of craftsmen and merchants, roughly similar to the one prior to the Turks, but with a Balkan, Oriental atmosphere.

The basis for industry was provided by the nearby mills. The Tettye brook played an important role. Mills stood on its banks and the Bosnian tanners, who arrived from the south, also worked here. They laid the foundations for the famous *leather industry* of Pécs. *Viticulture* was not destroyed under the Turks, moreover, it was enriched with new colours (Kadarka). The significance of the *wine and fruit trade* increased, despite the constant state of war.

The Oriental atmosphere of the town spread with the construction work. The Turks left the old houses untouched, but built floors of Oriental style above them, made of wood, and with windows protected by close screens. The old Christian churches were also transformed (Franciscan Church) or pulled down (St. Batholomew Church on the main square) replacing them with mosques. In fact the Turks built only mosques and baths. (The mosques of Pashas: Gazi Kassim, Hassan Jakovali, Ferhad and Elhaji Hussein.) The mosque (Franciscan church) of Pasha Memi within the Szigeti Gate and the djami of Sultan Suleiman in the Castle were also transformed churches. With the exception of the mosque of Gazi Kassim, the others were only minor prayer places. The Turks built two baths,

16

one on the corner of present-day Zetkin Klára and Kossuth Lajos streets (the bath of Pasha Ferhad) and the other on the corner of present-day Sallai and Várady Antal streets (the bath of Pasha Memi). The most luxurious bath—on the corner of Déryné street and Széchenyi square—was presumably extant in the Middle Ages, the Turks only changed its form. The major buildings were turned into monasteries, others into schools. For example, the Szatmáry residence at Tettye became a dervish monastery.

As mentioned earlier, the Hungarian population was pushed into the suburbs. They retained only one church: the All Saints church. Originally, it was jointly used by the various denominations. Later this unity was disrupted (1588: Pécs Dispute) and from that time on, they engaged in a life and death struggle. More than once the Turks had to pacify them. The Hungarians crowded into the suburbs, were constantly prone to the raids of the marauders, and occasionally (e. g. in 1603) to the attacks of the Tartar auxiliary troops "spending the winter" at Pécs, the free Heyducks on the run and the arbitrary Turkish overlords. Part of the Hungarian population were artisans, engaged in conventional trades, primarily working for the local Hungarian population and the neighbouring villages. A major part of them were engaged in agriculture on the estates of Turkish landowners near to the town. Some worked in vineyards or owned vineyards.

By the 1620s, the population of the town amounted to 5,000, however, this number was strongly reduced in the second half of the century. The declining Turkish Empire was not strong enough to protect the occupied towns, the forayers destroyed what they could, and did not spare the Hungarian population either. The 1664 campaign of Miklós Zrínyi, the poet and commander, launched one of the gravest periods in the history of the county. The devastation became complete, when in 1686 the army led by Louis of Baden, attacked Pécs and occupied it. By that time, the town was almost level with the ground on which it stood. With this, Turkish rule ended after 143 years.

THE MODERN HISTORY OF PÉCS

Pécs was liberated from under Turkish rule in a terrible condition. It could be said that no stone remained unturned in the town. Count Vecchi, the commander of the town, declared everything to be war booty and removed everything which could be taken. He took away the lead sheets from the cupola of the mosque, tore off all the tin taps of the Turkish baths, dug up the floor of the churches and searched for treasure even among the bones. In the meantime, he did not bother about the conquered "enemy"—mostly Hungarians. The population was almost left to starve to death.

In the main we can only presume what the town looked like after the withdrawal of the Turks, nevertheless, two important sources remain from that time. One was a *design* by military engineer Josef Haüy from 1687 on which he outlined the town and castle walls with passable accuracy. He also noted down the system of Pécs' fortification, the network of streets, and the Turkish buildings, mosques, baths and wells. The present-day and 17th century network of streets in Pécs are almost identical, there is only a sligth difference with regard to the period Main square (today Széchenyi square). Another very significant source is the large *County Register* from 1687, a part of which dealt with Pécs. The Register listed the intact and ruined houses of the town, and most important related facts. It provides surprising data. Despite the grave battles, several buildings remained intact or survived with little damage. These included 2 three leveled and 4 two leveled houses. The undamaged houses included 20 built of stone, 22 of wattle, and 21 of wood. There were 22 one roomed houses, 19 two roomed, 17 with 3 rooms and 13 with four or more rooms. Fifty-five of the buildings were covered with shingle, 5 were thatched, 2 with board and 2 with tiles. It can be said that these houses were very well built in the Middle Ages, before the Turkish times. Some of them are still extant. They were rebuilt and reshaped, given new facades, in baroque, then in romantic style, finally in ecletic style, but the interiors still reflect a medieval

18

atmosphere. An example of this is the two storey building in 17 Kossuth Lajos street, which was hardly damaged during the siege. At that time, the Royal Commissioner moved into the building.

After the expulsion of the Turks, life again started in the town, but soon another tragedy hit Pécs and its inhabitants. First in 1704, the *Kuruc*, then the *"Rác"* led by the imperial officers, devastated the town. According to period chronicles, following the ravages, the funerals lasted for 7 days. The next catastrophe was the Black Plague of 1710, which genuinely decimated the inhabitants of Pécs.

The 18th century history of the town was characterized by a very sharp fight against feudal restrictions. The burghers of the town, which started on the road towards economic development, launched an 80 year long struggle against the landlord, the Bishop, to gain the status of a free royal town. In fact, after the expulsion of the Turks, the Bishop immediately wanted to affectuate the feudal rights acquired in the Middle Ages. However, Emperor Leopold I did not return the town into his possession, but kept it under the administration of the Treasury. The citizens of the town of Pécs were pleased, because this practically hardly differed from what they wanted. However, in 1699 the Emperor promised to restore the rights of the Church, which was accomplished in 1703, and caused great consternation among the Pécs burghers. They unearthed all the genuine (even more forged) documents, with which they wished to prove that Ferdinand I had granted free royal rights to the town of Pécs already in 1528. However, nobody believed these documents, and the Bishop was the most suspicious. The Emperor did not believe them either, he obviously knew what was the truth, nevertheless, he did not completely refute the request, occasionally demanded by the Pécs burghers. True enough, he expected a lot of money for this. However, the process of affairs was very slow. Almost everybody had to be bribed, ranging from the clerks in the Chancellery to the Emperor.

In the meantime, emotions flew so freely in the town that both sides resorted to every tactic. Abuse, corruption and violence followed each other. Finally, György

Klimó, the enlightened Bishop, showed an inclination to satisfy the Pécs burghers, however, his hands were tied by the severe restrictions of the Vatican. In the end, the Queen (Maria Theresa) cut the Gordian knot by not appointing a new Bishop after the death of Klimó, before Pécs was granted its rights.

The town spent a lot of money, wine, hay and fodder until—after almost 80 years of struggle—the burghers attained their aim. In 1780 Pécs was granted the privileges of a *free royal town,* which was festively announced. Peace was established between the Bishop and the burghers of Pécs.

The town in debt slowly recovered and became economically strong. Its economic strength was ensured by the grapes and wine. It was no coincidence that the disputes always centred around the taverns. The Bishop, the chapter and the orders all wanted their share from the profit of the taverns. Naturally, the town wanted to acquire all of it.

Viticulture has long traditions at Pécs. It is sufficient to cast a glance at an old photograph or at an even older etching, where in the background extensive vineyards can be seen stretching along the slopes of the Mecsek down to the walls of the town. In addition to the known Arany hill, the Donatus, vineyards and orchards covered the side of the Makár mountain, the Frühweisz slopes, the eastern side of Kálvária hill, and the areas of the Csoronika, Szkokó, the Upper and Lower-Gyükés, Kispiricsizma, Szamárkút and Rigóder. The large amount of wine they produced could not be drunk at home. It had to be sold. A rivalry started. The wines of the church were not welcome, and the serving of alien wines was even more forbidden in the taverns.

After acquiring civil rights, the guilds underwent rapid expansion. One of the strongest guilds was that of the *tanners* (tabakosok), in the valley of the Tettye brook, in the area of the Tettye in Malom (Mill) street (9 Felsőmalom street). The craftsmen and merchants were mostly Germans, while Bosnians who lived around Barátur worked in the manufactures. As they were the poorest of Pécs society, they became the most radical revolutionaries of the political struggles, and

20

the most enthusiastic supporters of Kossuth in 1848, even under imperial occupation.

Cultural life developed in the second half of the 18th century, particularly under the bishopric of *György Klimó*. The progressive and enlightened bishop did a good deal to promote culture and sciences. In 1774, he opened his library with 15,000 volumes to the public, in 1773 he set up a paper mill and printing house, and a girls' school in 1776. However, he was unable to materialize his cherished plan, the restoration of the medieval Pécs university.

Coal which was discovered in the mid-18th century, had a major significance in the economic prosperitiy of Pécs, and coal started to be regularly mined from the mid-19th century. Coal was used locally as fuel from the 1840s onward. In 1844, the Limberger Sugar Refinery was set up, and a year later the Madarász iron plant (on the site of the present Leather Factory). The significance of coal continued to increase. János Náray, the bailiff of the Bishop, wrote about it in one of his articles in 1845: "In addition, coal is the great treasure of the town, which can be found all along the mountain in large quantities and one can believe that this will be the reason for the town's prosperity."

In the mid-19th century, the inhabitants of Pécs numbered 14,000. It was a small town; even in a Hungarian comparison, it was considered of medium size. Some etchings and pictures were preserved from those times, which enable us to guess what the town looked like at the end of the Reform Age. The etchings of Rochboch and Varoni depict a bright and friendly town. In the background, the forest covered Mecsek, with vineyards and orchards on its slopes, and a town bathing in the warm sunshine at the foot of the mountain. In 1815, Richard Bright, an English physician wrote the following about the town: "Observing Pécs from the south, one catches a fascinating view. It is situated on the side of a limestone ledge of rock. One or the other of the houses is conspicuously large, and as each of the churches have at least two small spires, similarly to the monasteries, the whole seems to be much bigger than a modestly built town of

21

hardly 9,000 inhabitants." Another traveller, Johann Gottfried Elsner, also wrote enthusiastically about the town 24 years later: "Towards dusk, I climbed the Calvary Hill, and looked down on the attractive landscape. The sun lit it up in a peculiar manner, an extremely pleasant scent covered it, which lent a certain magic to the entirety." The romantic tone roughly reflected the same atmosphere as the etchings. János Náray's article was much more practical. He was a local man, who also saw the problems very clearly: "The town of Pécs in built at the foothill on a slope and it's built day after day. New lines of houses are constructed, the streets are mostly paved with cobbles, but there is still a lot to be wished; the slopes suggest that without human hands, a good rain would sweep the streets, but the occasional underground sewers are also filled with mud. The streets are narrow and in an old fashioned way, disorderly, one house stands in, whilst another stands out ..."

The news about the March events of 1848 were brought by a boatman to Mohács, together with a copy of the National Song and the 12 points. These arrived in Pécs on March 18, where soon posters appeared on the streets: "Long live constitutional freedom!" and "Peaceful concord". The 12 points were read at the assembly meeting of the Town Council. The next day, the Town Council held a public meeting, where the 12 points were discussed and Freemen of the Town were elected, including Lajos Batthyány, Lajos Kossuth, Mihály Táncsics, Sándor Petőfi, Mihály Vörösmarty, István Széchenyi and József Eötvös.

In 1848—1849, Pécs only played a secondary role. The organisation of the defence line at the river Dráva was the assignment of Kázmér Batthyány, the Lord Lieutenant, then Government Commissioner appointed on April 22, a landlord of Baranya County of progressive outlook. Although he declared a popular rising, the events followed each other so rapidly that even this was insufficient to assemble a considerable force to the Dráva line. Between September 17—19, 1848 part of Jellasics' army, commanded by generals Róth and Philippovič crossed the Dráva at Sellye and unobstructed advanced towards Pécs. On September 24, the troops occupied the town without a fight, then left it moving towards the north, and proceeded towards Buda via Székesfehérvár. This army was disarmed at Ozora by the National Guard, and its rear echelon and ammunition were captured on September 27, at Oroszlán by the Pécs National Guard, and seized it as war booty.

Although the Imperial troops moved into Pécs on January 31, 1849 and immediately introduced a state of emergency in the town, the resistance of the population could not be broken. The poor of the Budai suburb and primarily the Bosnians constantly harassed the occupying enemy. After the Imperial troops left Pécs, the revolutionaries united with the soldiers of the national army, who arrived in Pécs on June 12, and attempted resistance, nevertheless, the enemy again occupied the town almost without a struggle. This put an end to the revolutionary and war activities at Pécs, but the revolution left deep imprints in the people. For a long time, Pécs was in the vanguard of left-wing movements. Many people recalled the 1848—1849 events as a permanent reminder.

Absolutism oppressed the Hungarian people as a grave tribulation. The situation was also difficult at Pécs. A military magistrate arrived in the town and he even brought a hangman with him. The military court started its activity, and several buildings were turned into prisons. In 1852, Emperor Franz Joseph travelled through Pécs during his tour of the country. The lackeys of the counter-revolutionary system received the oppressor of freedom with great reverence.

Despotism obstructed progress, but could not stop it for ever. In the 1850s, the economic life of Pécs started to develop, first slowly, then more rapidly. Factories and plants were set up one after the other, slowly Pécs turned into an industrial town.

1850: First Pécs Lime and Brick Factory
1852: Imre Zsolnay's Pottery
1853: Scholz' Brewery, and Hirschfeld (Pannonia) Brewery
1858: Weidinger Steam Mill
1859: Littke Champagne Plant

1861: Hamerli Glove Factory
1862: Adolf Engel Parquet Factory
1867: Angster Organ Factory, and
1868: Zsolnay Factory.

The industrial boom was due to coal mining. After having discovered coal in 1769, the mining rights were partly bought, partly rented by the First Danube Steam Shipping Society (DGT) in 1853. Production was carried out with increasing intensity, and the company settled and employed Moravian, Bohemian, Krainian, Styrian, Serbian, Croatian, Tyrolean, Carinthian, Italian, and German workers. While in 1853, only 53 workers were employed, this number increased to 774 in 1860, to 1,705 in 1870, to 2,753 in 1880, to 2,613 in 1890, and to 4,021 in 1900. The miners lived in colonies set up by the DGT at Pécsbánya, Vasas and Meszes. They were proper industrial workers, many of them already organised in unions, pioneers of the strike movement. From the 1880s onwards, their struggles for higher wages acquired national significance.

In 1888, then in 1907 major industrial fairs were held at Pécs. The one in 1907 was of national significance. The glittering pavilions on the extensive site of the exhibition were visited by hundreds of thousands of people. The celebrations also included the unveiling of the statue of *Vilmos Zsolnay*, the great factory founder. At the beginning of the 20th century, Pécs was a Hungarian town of medium size, with important industry, an extending mining area and an organised, large scale industrial working class.

At the end of the First World War, Pécs became a centre of the anti-war movement. On May 20, 1918 the 6th Battalion of the 6th Infantry Regiment temporarily stationed in the barracks on Irányi Dániel square was ordered to the front. The 3rd Auxiliary Company refused to obey the order and being armed appealed to the other units and the miners to join them. The number of insurgents was almost 1,700. Later about 150 armed miners joined them. They fought against the units ordered to move against them, but the rebellion was oppressed and the leaders were

24

executed. However, the revolutionary mood did not cease to boil in the town. In 1918, the National Council was elected at Széchenyi square with great enthusiasm. Workers' Councils were set up in the factories. The enfolding revolutionary wave was broken by the Entente-Serbian troops, who moved into the town on October 18, 1918. The entire society of Pécs protested against the occupation, and against the persecution of progressive ideas. After the overthrow of the Hungarian Republic of Councils in 1919, the policy of the occupiers suddenly changed. Seemingly they made peace with the earlier persecuted left-wing. During that period—when White Terror engaged in a frenzy in Hungary and the left-wing movements were also persecuted on the area of the Serbian Kingdom—the revolutionary forces were allowed to enfold in this occupied territory, and were even supported. The unconcealed aim was the annexation of the area (and Pécs), and this policy was pursued for this end. The occupation came to an end on August 20, 1921 when Horthy's troops marched into Pécs. The only positive feature of the occupation was that the left-wing movement could freely enfold at Pécs, and in 1919 Pécs avoided the blood bath of the White Terror. However, the Horthy regime did not forgive Pécs for its left-wing attitude during the occupation. The years of crisis were grave and strikes and protest demonstrations followed each other. One of the bloodiest events of the period between the two world wars was the great hunger strike in 1937, when the gendarmes shot the unarmed protesting miners af Csertető. Three died and several demonstrators were wounded.

During the Second World War, Pécs belonged among the fortunate towns. Neither air raids nor ground battles damaged the town.

THE CENTRE OF SOUTH TRANSDANUBIA

Pécs was liberated on November 29, 1944. However, the battle for the town started days earlier. The Germans did not want to give up the town without a struggle, and when they were unable to hold it any

25

longer, they wanted to annihilate the station, factories, plants and mines. However, the workers prevented the devastation. The Soviet troops—to spare the town—started the attack from several directions. In order to prevent encirclement, the German and Hungarian troops withdrew from Pécs. The day after the liberation, life was restarted, and production commenced in the factories. The leaders almost completely independently started to democratize life in the county and town.

The political struggles of the 1940s did not avoid Pécs. The Independent Smallholders' Party was rather strong in the county, while at Pécs the workers' parties strengthened. The Social Democratic Party was stronger in the factories and the Communist Party among the miners. The communists had a decisive role in the organisation of the work, in the battle for coal, in the reconstruction of the destroyed Dráva area, and in providing support for Budapest and Székesfehérvár.

Before the liberation, Pécs was a genuine Hungarian provincial town, with medium sized light industry and significant coal mining. Culture, education, and scientific life reached good standards. A guarantee of this was the university, resettled from Pozsony to Pécs, the Transdanubian Scientific Institute set up in the 1940s, two museums and the archives, the company of the Pécs National Theatre with an eminent cast, and high level musical life.

As Pécs survived the war intact—in contrast to other Hungarian towns—development could start more easly, which however, with the exception of coal mining, was rather slow until the beginning of the 1950s. The first major step forward started in the mid-1950s. In addition to the coal mines, ore mines were opened that resulted in a further increase in the working class. Extensive construction work started. The Meszes township was built, then Újmecsekalja (more popularly called the Uranium town) replaced the old airfield, military drill ground and race course. Finally, in the 1970s, building work also started in the Suburb (Kertváros), which was named after Lvov, the sister town of Pécs. In the meantime, the new town centre was built on the site of former Pajta street and later

Majláth street, with its public institutions, modern network of shops, and broad arenue, which solved the almost deadlocked traffic of Pécs, providing access for the traffic crossing the town.

Pécs was always a town of schools. Before the liberation, 4 secondary schools, 2 technical schools, and a university first with 3 and later with 2 departments justified this description. By 1980, the number of general schools had incdeased to 36, the apprentice training schools to 3, and that of grammar and vocational secondary schools to 12 (plus 1 commerce secondary school). High level education also underwent a major improvement. Today, Pécs has several universities and high schools. The *Janus Pannonius University of Arts* (preceded by the Pécs University of Arts) was set up in 1982. Tuition is carried out in 3 departments: state and legal sciences, economics, and the teachers' training faculty. The Pécs *Medical University* has 2 departments: general medical sciences and dental sciences. In 1970, two high level technical schools were merged and the *Mihály Pollack Technical High School* was set up with 2 departments: engineering and building industry, where factory engineers are trained. Primarily teachers of singing and music are trained at the local branch of the Budapest *Ferenc Liszt Academy of Music.*

High standard artistic and scientific life have old traditions at Pécs. The task of the Pécs Academy Committee (PAB), set up in 1969, is the co-ordination of the scientific life in South Transdanubia (Baranya, Somogy, Tolna and Zala Counties). For this end, 8 special committees organise scientific work, and also contribute to national research themes. Within the framework of the PAB, considerable local and national research work is carried out at the Pécs Medical University. The research work—covering the fields of the technical sciences—handled in the Mecsek Coal Mines, in the Mecsek Ore Mining Company and in the Mihály Pollack Technical High School, should not be neglected either.

A centre of social scientific research work is the *Transdanubian Scientific Institute of the Hungarian Academy of Sciences,* where economic and social re-

27

search is carried out concerning Pécs and South Trans-danubia. In the past 15 years, considerable results were also archived in the sphere of historic sciences. The *Baranya County Archives* are the workshop of the historic sciences, where the joint work of urban and county history researchers resulted in significant scientific achievements. In addition to the annually published Baranya Local History, the planned series of 24 volumes of the Baranya Monography are organised and edited by the Baranya County Archives. This is a unique undertaking of national significance. The Archives co-ordinate the chronicle, which covers every settlement of the county, and—which alone in Hungary—gathered and evaluates the political, economic, cultural, demographic and other data of the villages and towns from the aspect of the local chronicler, namely, from the viewpoint of the small communities of the settlements—since 1971.

Literary life was always exhilarated by the magic of the landscape, the situation of the town and its pleasant climate. Hungarian literature started out from Pécs in the Middle Ages. The first Hungarian writer was Mór, the Bishop of Pécs. This was also where Janus Pannonius lived, the humanist poet of European significance. After the expulsion of the Turks, the multilingual physiognomy of the town did not favour Hungarian language literature. The first genuine upswing came in the 20th century. After the liberation an effervescent literary life developed. Writers and poets of national significance created here, or started out on their literary career. At present, the artistic and literary publication "Jelenkor" (Present Age) co-ordinates the literary life of Baranya and Pécs.

Pécs is considered the town of arts. Artists were always pleased to settle here, because they were not only attracted by the magic milieu and the attractive town, but also by the patronage of the arts. In the first half of the century, Ernő Gebauer, Jenő Gábor, Géza Nikelszky, then Ferenc Martyn, Béla Simon, Sándor Rétfalvy, Ilona Fürtös, Ferenc Lantos and János Bizse, the members of the "Pécs Workshop" created flourishing artistic life at Pécs. They appeared in public with frequent exhibitions, and their works are

28

also on display at the permanent exhibitions of the Janus Pannonius Museum.

Dramatic arts also have long traditions at Pécs. The list of the great old actors and actresses includes Mrs. Déry, and Endre Latabár's famous company also appeared here. In the 1940s and 1950s, the company of the Pécs National Theatre included Ferenc Bessenyei, Zsuzsa Gordon, György Kálmán and István Avar. For a time, the Theatre was managed by József Szendrő. At present, a musical company operates beside the drama company. The *Pécs Ballet* was set up in 1960, which since then acquired international fame. Pécs became the citadel of modern ballet. The *Bóbita Puppet Ensemble,* which acquired national renown in the 1970s, is the youngest company of the Pécs National Theatre. As a new initiative, the basis of a *summer theatrical festival series* was laid down in 1978. The great success resulted in the foundation of the *Pécs Summer Theatre,* the co-ordinator of multidirectional theatre experiments.

The outstanding music life also has century-old traditions at Pécs. The German and Bohemian burghers who settled in the town after the Turkish times, brought their appreciation of music with them. The bishops of the town were particularly careful to ensure that the musicians, conductors and organists of the Cathedral should be first class masters of their art. In addition to high level ecclesiastic music, secular music was always of major significance. Prosper Amtmann (1809—1854), the world famous flute artist who was born at Sellye, spent the last years of his life at Pécs. Imre Weidinger (1792—1859) the renowned bassoonist also settled at Pécs, in his birthplace, at the end of his long European concert tour. János Gungl and György Lickl, composer and conductor, as well as violinist János Witt spent a long time at Pécs. Dezső Ernster, the world famous singer of the Metropolitan Opera, was a son of Pécs. In the latter part of his life, he appeared at several memorial concerts in Pécs. The Pécs Choir set up in 1862, worthily represented the standards of Pécs' musical life. During its existence, it gave several outstanding concerts and won major prizes. It was one of the most famous choirs of Hungary. Present musical life is determined by the educational activity of the Ferenc Liszt Academy of Music. The traditional choir movement still flourishes at Pécs. The *Ferenc Liszt Choir*, the Chamber Choir of the House of Teachers' at Pécs, is also known beyond the frontiers of Hungary. The *school choirs* (Dobó István, Széchenyi István and Nagy Lajos grammar schools) are acquiring an increasing good name.

The *Pécs Philharmonic Orchestra*, under the baton of conductors of national and international fame, regularly gives noteworthy concerts.

IMPRESSIONS OF PÉCS

From which ever direction we arrive in Pécs, there is a point on the road directly in front of the town, from where the panorama of the county seat opens up with unexpected charm. First only the Television Tower's outline appears on the skyline, then the blueish-grey Misina, the Tubes, the Jakab, Makár and Havi mountains tower high, the latter with its blinding white walled little church. And then, the town built on the slope of the mountain comes into view. It is a fascinating spectacle and always different. Which ever part of the year or the day we arrive, Pécs always shows a different face. Although rarely —in clear weather—the walls of the houses light up like lamps, the roofs are clear-cut, and one can see even the minute details of the chimneys. On such occasions, the sparkling lights and the dark, almost black shadows playfully alternate.

In the summer sunshine, the town bathes in warm colours. Beside the deep green of the Mecsek, the colours glow. Former travellers and designers considered this peaceful and warm atmosphere the most miraculous spectacle of Pécs, this is what they wrote about and what they painted. Although today, it is mostly clad in fog and smoke, the panorama is fascinating even in this gloomy smog. The details disappear and fade away, and the town melts into the wonderful milieu, it unites with it.

The town is different in the winter, or in October in the colourful framework of the autumn Mecsek side. It is different in the morning, enfolding from the fog, and in the evening, lit up by thousands of small lamps. Which ever direction we approach it, it is always different.

It is beautiful for those who grumble, because slowly the town grows beyond the opportunities pro-

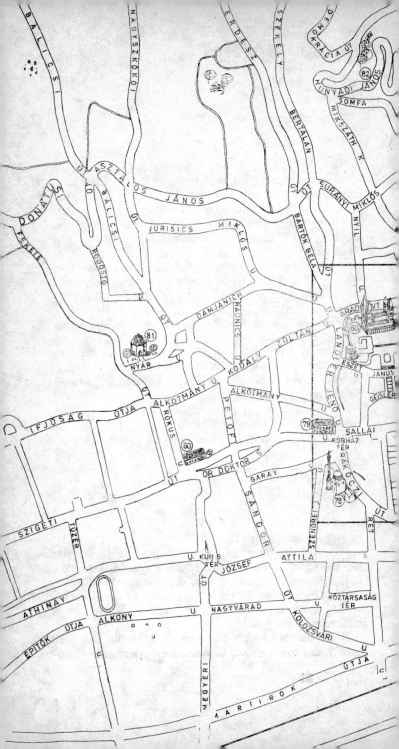

vided by the vicinity, and for those who are not impressed by the numerous almost completely identical concrete cubes replacing the old, romantic and run-down houses, and beautiful for those who grind their teeth when losing their way in the one-way labyrinth of the inner-city, or who consider the old musty abode houses in the Budai suburb as miserable and ripe to be swept away. And also for those who are irritated by the Television Tower, the Glove Factory or the skyscraping slab of a 23 storeyed building. At the gateway to Pécs, the panorama is equally attractive for the Pécs citizens and for guests on their way to Pécs.

The writer has to say the following:

"When one comes from the direction of Harkány and reaches the hill above the cemetery, after the airfield, one suddenly and unexpectedly catches the lights of the town. The road slowly descends into the valley, and the horizon fills up with tiny lights from the east to west. The lamps wink intimately, they come always closer and when you reach the deepest point of the valley, suddenly the picture disappears..."

"The night lights of the town are most beautiful perhaps from the mountain. I am sitting on the white limestone cliffs of the Havi mountain with the town below me. It is as if I sat on the Italian or Spanish coast and lights flash up under the water. The creases of the mountain cast bays and protrusions, the chimneys of the Power Plant stand out like light houses. The tied down buoys of the street lamps light up lilac atolls—tiled houses. Between the underwater islands the fluorescent bodies of fish—the buses. One can only guess the line of streets, marked by the line of pearls of lights..." (Tibor Tüskés)

A The general map of Pécs

A STROLL THROUGH THE INNER-CITY

The old former wall embraced inner-city of Pécs has 42 streets and 6 squares. These include the passages: Boltív (Vault) köz and Megye (County) köz, etc., and among the squares Flórián tér without any numbered house. In fact most of the streets already existed in the Middle Ages. The "new" ones were usually built in the 19th century, after breaking through the town walls: Bástya (1861), Bercsényi (1905), Meredek (1839), Esze Tamás (1787) streets and Hal (Fish) square (1806). Streets were also opened in the inner-city alongside gardens and empty plots: Eötvös (1881), Goldmark Károly (1910) and Toldi Miklós (1938) streets and Tanácsház (Council Hall) passage (1907). One of the oldest is Káptalan (Chapter) street.

The Eötvös street "lived" for the shortest time, although it still exists, only it is much shorter and is reduced to a cul de sac.

In the past, careful attention was paid to ensuring that where the street crossed the town wall and later the district limits—it should have a different name. An example of this is Kossuth Lajos street, which started at Sörház (Brewery) street, because the stretch towards Fő (Main) square was called Király (King) street. The site of the present Hunyadi road was earlier the very narrow Inczédy Dénes street, but only up to the former Castle Gateway, from there it was called Kaposvári street, obviously commemorating the gateway leading to Kaposvár.

The medieval names of the streets are not known. Some clues are provided by Turkish tax records, although they occasionally gave one name for whole districts. In 1554, the following street names were noted down: Szent Ferenc (St. Francis), Kiss Kőhid (Little Stone bridge), Szent Tamás (St. Thomas), Nagy (Big), Német (German), Fazekas (Potter), Piac (Market), and Szent Mária (St. Mary). Unfortunately, the list does not reveal which of them was in the inner-city, and which outside the walls. During the 150 years of Turkish occupation, many streets were renamed. We know the names: Omer aga, Ali Effendi, Dervis bég and Martalóc streets.

Present-day Széchenyi square was earlier more a street than a square. At the time the Turks were driven out, it was called Négycsatornya (Four channel) street.

Later, in keeping with the changing times, the names also changed. When Pécs came under German influence, the streets were given German names, which were later translated into Hungarian, an example of this is the Schuler Gasse—Iskola (School) utca. Streets were named after saints, politicians, personalities or crafts and this continued until recent times.

Three suburbs evolved during the centuries around the historic inner-city of Pécs. First the Budai suburb, which remained almost up to our times the industrial district of the town, then the Szigeti suburb, and finally the Siklósi suburb. While the network of streets developed already in the Middle Ages, in the inner-city—surrounded by walls—essentially no change occurred, in the suburbs only a few or no streets developed for long centuries.

The most ancient settlement of the Budai suburb evolved around the All Saints Church, and along the Tettye brook, which always abounded in water, mills alternated with the tanneries along the whole stretch. Houses were built on major or minor plots. They could only be approached via narrow alleyways, passages or steps. Those who were not familiar with the neighbourhood were confronted with walls or fences, or ended up in cul de sacs, and even if they found the exit through the winding thoroughfares, they had difficulties in reaching their place of destination.

Those who belonged to the same nationality or the same trade usually lived in one group. Little townships, independent, separated small settlements and considerably closed communities developed in the suburbs. These small islands of settlements preserved their separate identity until the 20th century. An example of this was one of the most ancient settlements, dating back to Turkish times, called the "Neighbourhood of Barátur". This is how the former tenants called it, not giving street names, which was impossible as there was not one street in it. This "island" was only divided into streets in 1926. "Puturluk" under the Tettye was a well known "island". Similarly to the Neighbourhood of Barátur, it was populated by Bosnians. Later, it was divided into two streets: Lower and Upper Puturluk streets (today: Vince and Majthényi Ferenc streets). The "Benga" was in the area of Andy Endre, Katalin and Könyök streets, initially a closed settlement without streets. The „Zidina" area was also similar, and its name is still extant. The former "Józsafát valley" was situated alongside the present Hunyadi János and Aradi vértanúk (Martyrs of Arad) roads. The area—full of vineyards and orchards—was given this name in the 1850s or 1860s. Two such "islands" without streets were set up in the Szigeti suburb. At the beginning of our century, these two areas were still called "Kisgyűd" and "Rókusalja".

These characteristic Pécs curiosities ceased when the official street arrangement took place. This was the time when the town was divided into districts. Street signs appeared on the walls, and initially the street name signs were of different colours, depending on the district. The inner-city was white, the Budai surburb green, the Szigeti suburb blue, and the Siklósi suburb was red. The letters and numbers were black on the coloured sign boards.

The first printed town maps were published in 1864, and the different districts were marked with the same colours.

SZÉCHENYI SQUARE

The History of the Square

For centuries, the main square of Pécs was the centre of the town. After the Tartar invasion, the settlement was surrounded by walls and the role of the square increased. There was access to the town from four directions through 4 gateways. The four main roads met in the middle, where 2 squares of irregular shape developed. Even the superficial observer recognizes that there are 2 squares, a "lower" and an "upper" one. In the Middle Ages, this was even more so, for there was a block of houses around the present Trinity Statue before the expulsion of the Turks, and the 2 squares were linked by a street named—as mentioned earlier—Fourchannel street. (Most probably Market Street mentioned in the 16th century "defter" referred to the same.)

The St. Bertalan Church, built in an east-west direction, stood in the middle of the "upper" square. (It was first mentioned in documents dating from 1309.)

The Main square always had a significant function, partly as an ecclesiastic centre and partly as a junction at the meeting point of the main roads coming from 4 directions, which became the resting place of the merchants. A market developed here, a genuine trading centre. In the Middle Ages, several significant trading routes passed through Hungary. One of them, the one between Byzantium and Regensburg also touched upon Pécs, which had a considerable effect on the development of the town. The fairs and markets were administered by the town authorities, they also collected the fair and market dues, etc. It is no coincidence that in towns the administrative centres —the town halls—were usually built on the market square. Pécs was no exception.

In the early Hungarian Middle Ages, the square was roughly in the geometric centre of the area surrounded by walls. However, this was not identical with the centre of the dwelling houses. The medieval town was more to the east of the square. The ecclesiastic buildings and areas of the episcopal town were situated to the west of the square. The episcopal castle was situated in the north-west corner of the town, together with the auxiliary buildings of the bishop, surrounded by the houses of the chapter and it may have been the site of the medieval university, and the gardens and orchards of the bishop and chapter. The main square seemed to separate the civil and ecclesiastic town. Very few events of the Middle Ages are known, but most probably all of them took place on this square.

After 1543, a major change occurred in the Main square. The Turks pulled down the Gothic triple naved St. Bertalan Church, and used the stones to build the mosque of Gazi Kassim (Victorious Kassim—the first Sanjak Bey of Pécs). The mosque faced Mecca, with a public fountain in front of it, and a bath to the east. Turkish vendors and merchants settled in the square, the atmosphere was busy, noisy and Oriental. Urban life flourished in the High street and in the Main square between the bazaars, which occupied almost every little space. The crowd flowed between them, and the extensive djami towered over the colourful multitude with stately grace, with its lead covered cupola and slim minaret.

In the 18th century, the square already acquired a Baroque character. The buildings from Turkish times were either pulled down or reconstructed. Between 1727 and 1731, the Capuchin Church and monastery was built in the southern part of the square. This area was earlier sold to the Pécs Chapter by Imre Tabak. The deed from 1695 is extant, Imre Tabak signed in Turkish. Obviously, he was one of those Mohammedan Bosnians who was converted to Christianity, and settled in Pécs.

The atmosphere of the square was provided by the Jesuit priory (today: Asztalos Students' Hostel), the mosque—rebuilt in a Baroque style—and the two level Town Hall. The eastern side of the square was lined by the Turkish bath, and to the south of it—the rectory. Later, it was replaced by a new rectory alongside the old one. At that time, the square was built in a zig-zag, with the fire station and tiny shops, which extended to the Fő utca (High street). On the other side of the square, the Cséby House in Baroque style and the Czindery House in Louis XVI style—stood to the south of the priory—a Jesuit building until 1733. Their noble lines distinguished them from the similar private buildings of Pécs.

The Trinity statue already stood in the middle of the square at the beginning of the 18th century, therefore, it was also named Szentháromság tér

(Trinity square). The statue was replaced at the beginning of the 19th century by a statue of András Berchardt and in 1908 by a creation of György Kiss. Two fountains in a Baroque style replaced the earlier Turkish fountains on the square. One—south from the entrance to the Town Hall—was built in 1701. The upper fountain, situated between the Trinity statue and the entrance to the church, was built in 1709—1710. Both fountains were removed at the end of the 19th century. These fountains were interesting spots on the Main square, with life whirling around them. The neighbourhood was noisy in the early morning with the rattle of the watering carts, the chatting of the maids collecting water and the cries of the market vendors.

Pécs was liberated from under the feudal yoke in 1780 and with this the hardest obstacle was removed from the path towards economic prosperity. Under the effervescent effect of the Reform Age, Pécs was built into the centre of South Trandanubia in the 19th century. New buildings were erected on the still chaotic main square by the well-to-do burghers of the town (Piatsek, Littke and Zsolnay). In 1804, the Turkish baths were pulled down and replaced by the two storeyed building of the later Burghers' Casino. József Piatsek, built his two storeyed corner house at the beginning of the century (Széchenyi tér 8.).

In 1830, the building of a new Town Hall started on the site of the demolished two storeyed building. The designs of the three storeyed spired building in a classicist style were made in Vienna, and József Piatsek was entrusted with the building work. The noble construction was one of the finest among the town halls in Hungary.

The simple Eiser House in a classicist style (today: 2nd district wedding hall), was completed in 1840, then in 1845 the Nádor Hotel and below it three so-called "merchants' houses". With this the square became almost completely built up and perhaps it was never so unified and attractive than at that time. The last significant construction of that period was the Taizs House, built around 1860, in a romantic style.

In the Reform Age, during the 1848 revolution and

War of Independence, the main square became the centre of political life. The revolutionaries gathered here on March 19, 1848 when the news of the Pest uprising was announced and the 12 points read. This is where the news about the results of the struggle and battles arrived. The revolution was of short duration at Pécs, the imperial troops marched into the town and lined up on the square. From that time onward the inhabitants cheering Kossuth clashed here with the imperial occupiers and this is where the revolutionaries were flogged. Bishop Scytovsky of Pécs, then archbishop of Esztergom, held a thanks-giving service in the inner-city Church, when the Emperor crushed the revolution, and the progressive intellectuals of the nobility and burghers demonstrated on the square against German language theatre performances and called for the use of the Hungarian language, and this is where Emperor Franz Josef I was received when he visited Pécs.

In the 20th century, the square—already called Széchenyi—became the everyday venue of the most important events of the town. In 1907, the builders stopped work during the construction of the new Town Hall and with this the working class movement also made its entry onto the square. The National Council was declared here on October 31, 1918 and this marked the victory of the bourgeois democratic revolution in Pécs. However, no further progress could take place, because on November 14, 1918 the Serbian Royal Army occupied the town. The occupying soldiers lined up on Széchenyi square. During the years of the occupation, large numbers of political events took place on the square. Demonstrations during the general strike (February—March 1919), then against the counter-revolutionary system and against the arrival of the counter-revolutionary troops. The "leading committee" of the Pécs Socialist Party operated here, and the Baranya—Baja Serbian—Hungarian Republic was declared here on August 14, 1921.

However, on August 20, 1921 the troops of the counter-revolutionary regime marched into Pécs. General Soós inspected the troops at Széchenyi square. Governor Horthy also came to visit. Counter-revolution

41

settled in the town, exactly on the square, thus becoming the centre of the right-wing forces.

During the Second World War, the Volksbund, the organisation of Germans in Hungary, held its mass meeting here, when it became clear that they considered the town and Baranya, part of the "Great German Empire".

On November 29, 1944 Pécs was liberated. Széchenyi square became the symbol of democratic transformation. The first parade of the Pécs garrison of the democratic army was held here. The festive session also took place here, when the end the war was declared.

Between 1945 and 1948, the square was the venue of fierce party struggles. The various parties held their election and political meetings almost exclusively on the square. This was also the venue of the major May Day demonstrations. From among the significant political and social events, the 1961 visit of Yuri Gagarin, the first cosmonaut of the world should be mentioned. If one compares a photograph taken in the 1870s with a current snap, the former main square can hardly be recognized. The Town Hall was demolished, together with the Czindery and Cséby Houses, the Nádor Hotel and the school (today: Innercity School); the Piatsek House, the Oertzen House (today: County Court), the Inner-city Church, the centre of the square were reconstructed. The two public fountains disappeared, together with the trees nad the market stalls. There are no longer any tempting coffee-houses, horse-drawn cabs, gas lamps and the tram, which was introduced in 1913, also only exists in reminiscences.

At the turn of the century, the eclectic style appeared with all its exaggerations. The Town Hall, the Savings Bank (today: an office block), the Lóránt Palace, and the new Nádor Hotel with its flashy character—upset the balance of the square, and oppressed the atmosphere of the simple, noble lines of the baroque and classicist buildings.

Nevertheless, Széchenyi square is still a fascinating ensemble. Its well arranged buildings are high ranking fine lined art monuments. The Mecsek provides a pretty backcloth, with the interesting mosque cupola.

Spectacles of the Square

1 B   **Council Hall.** The present building of the Council Hall, the former Town Hall, was built at the beginning of the 20th century in an eclectic style. Its style and immense mass does not fit into the historic town centre, it clashes with the intimate, small town atmosphere of the square. It replaced the old—much smaller Town Hall—in 1907. The present is the third building during the post-Turkish history of Pécs. It was not kniwn when the first was built, perhaps immediately after the expulsion of the Turks, maybe at the beginning of the 18th century. It was a two storeyed baroque style building, with a small turret on its northern wing, and tiny shops on the ground floor, with two baroque vaulted gateways. The small balcony with iron railing above the gateway to the High street (Kossuth Lajos utca), opened from the conference room. According to archive records: the pillory stood on the corner, and lower down the public fountain built at the beginning of the century.

The building was the centre of the struggle for patent rights. Both the conference room on the first floor and the tavern on the groundfloor played an equally important role in these struggles. In fact wine and taverning were the basis for the prosperity of the town, and the main income of the landlord. For almost 100 years, this was the basis for disputes. After attaining the patent (1780), the town rapidly prospered. The "noble town" became autonomous, and the old Town Hall became too small for the administration. Small and meagre. The Town Council decided to build a new one, the designs were ordered from Vienna in 1829, and the building was entrusted to József Piatsek, the outstanding architect of the town. Piatsek surveyed the old building (fortunately, because an authentic and accurate design remained), then he demolished the building and started on the construction of the new Town Hall. It was completed in 1834. There are photographs of that building in addition to the original designs. It was a three level turreted building in a classicist style, one the finest of our provincial town halls.

The coat-of-arms of the town were placed into the tympanon of the central projection of the main entrance. A similar projection was built at the side entrance to the High street, but instead of a tympanon, a slender turret was built with a balcony and clock. Both projections were decorated by four Ionic pillars.

As the time passed, the building proved to be too small, with insufficient room for the offices. The Town Council pondered over the transformation for many years, then when the decision could no longer be delayed, a competition was held to design a new Town Hall. As a result, the old building was demolished, and the building of the new Town Hall commenced, based on the designs of Adolf Lang (1906). With this, one of the finest art monuments of the town disappeared.

The present building was completed in 1907, it is a three storeyed building in ecclectic style, with a *clock tower* over its northern facade, and a circular balcony. The eastern facade opens onto the Tanácsház köz (Town Hall alley). The alley was opened in 1907, during the building work.

The northern and western parts of the groundfloor are occupied by Pécs' first department store, the *Centrum department store*. The *Tourist Office* is situated next to the main entrance.

B Széchenyi Square

1. Council Hall
2. Lóránt Palace
3. No. 2 Surgical Clinic
4. Sárkány House
5. Széchenyi tér 7.
6. Piatsek House
7. The former building of the Pécs Savings Bank
8. "Asztalos János" Secondary School Students' Hostel
9. The former Országh House
10. 2nd district wedding hall

11. Baranya County Court
12. Nádor Hotel
13. The former Zsolnay House
14. Inner-city Church
15. Trinity statue
16. The mounted statue of János Hunyadi
17. Vilmos Zsolnay memorial fountain
18. "Elephant block"
19. Zsolnay centenary memorial fountain
53. School building

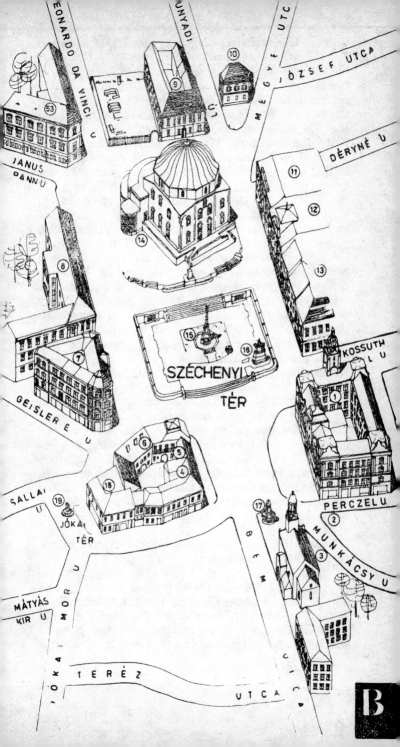

2 B **Lóránt Palace** (Széchenyi tér 2.). It is named after its original owner. In 1883, it was built on 4 bordering plots. The best known building was the two storeyed Baroque corner house, with a garret on top, called by the Pécs people: "Patkányvár" (Rat Castle). The reason for this nickname may have been the dilapidated state of the building in the second half of the century. Most probably the locals were ashamed of it, because hardly any photographs made at that time depicted the building, and great care was taken when photographing the Town Hall to avoid the "Rat Castle". Despite the fact that it was a characteristic example of the Pécs Baroque architecture and its former tenants must have been interesting people, characteristic Pécs burghers. The last owner, Dr. Lipót Loewy (Lóránt) pulled down the dilipated house and replaced it with the present "palace". During the demolition, a stone with a coat-of-arms was found built into the wall of the old house. Many people reckoned that it belonged to the former university. Half of the stone, found in two pieces, was taken by Antal Horváth, later the founder of the Museum, and by the time he sent for the second piece it was already built into the new wall. On the ground-floor of the new building, Scheffer opened the Central Coffee-house on November 24, 1888, it soon became a favourite meeting point and was renamed in 1904 the Balaton coffee-house. The "Two crown" restaurant (1905) on the Perczel street wing was renamed: the Workers' Casino in 1913. The publican was József Pécs, who also played a significant role in the working class movement. The owner set up studios on the upper floor and renowned photographers worked here. This was the first building in Pécs with a lift.

Today, the *No. 1 Pharmacy* takes the place of the former café and restaurant.

3 B **No. 2 Surgical Clinic** (former monastery and church of the Good Samaritans, Széchenyi tér 4—5.). The oldest and most interesting deed and document of the town is connected with the plot on which the building stood: Imre Tabak (obviously a

46

tanner, a Bosnian of Turkish origin) sold his house and plot in 1695 to the Paulites. In 1698, the Capuchins moved here and onto the neighbouring plots. Their church was consecrated in 1727. In 1734, the monks built the still extant western chapel at the western part of the church. The monastery was built in 1731. In 1786, Emperor Joseph II dissolved the order. Until 1796, the building served secular purposes, when János György Krautszak, a reputed miller and tanner of Pécs, set up a foundation of 25,000 forints, and the order of the Good Samaritans could open a hospital in the building, and constructed a pharmacy beside the church. Later, a separate hospital wing was added. The Good Samaritans built apartment houses and public buildings on their plot. They continuously extended their hospital and restored the church, which originally had a wooden tower. In 1891, the northern facade was rebuilt in neo-renaissance style, based on the designs of Ágoston Kirstein.

In 1908, Ede Graits, a local painter, decorated the vault of the church interior with Tiepolo copies.

The *Mary statue,* by György Kiss, can be seen in the niche above the entrance. The relief of *Pious St. John* by Ede Mayer, was placed on the Bem street church wall in 1905. The square ended *sanctuary, inlaid wooden altars* and the open *belfry* are of special interest.

The monastery has an ambulatory and a small courtyard in the middle, with a *carved stone framed cellar entrance,* a *fountain with wall basin,* and an ornamental *signal bell.*

At present, the building belongs to the No. 2 Surgical Clinic of the POTE (Pécs Medical University).

4 B   **Sárkány (Dragon) House** (Széchenyi tér 6.). The house was named after its former owner, Dr. Ármin Sárkány, a lawyer, later Police Commissioner. The present eclectic form of the building developed at its renovation in 1893. In 1974—1975, the building was completed restored. The attractive *wrought iron railing* of the balcony and the gateway decorated with a dragon were renewed.

The core of the building is of medieval origin. The

first data originate from 1713: a goldsmith bought the remnants of a burnt down house. The house may have perished during the Turkish war or during the so-called devastation of the "Rác". Its alternating owners, among them high ranking aristocrats, such as Count Schmidegg and Count László Esterházy, may have rebuilt and extended the building on several occasions. The *medieval wing* still exists on the southern side, in the courtyard of the building. The four massive stone pillars and the vaulted corridor allow us to presume that it may have been an arcaded house in the Middle Ages. Unfortunately, the unparalleled interesting building did not attract the attention of restorers, although this is one of the most valuable medieval architectural relics of Pécs.

5 B **Széchenyi tér 7.** The building was owned by noblemen of Pécs and Baranya in 1712 (Zombory, Hoits, and Kajdatsi). In 1822, it was bought by János Mihály Schönherr, the first owner of the Nádor Hotel.

The two storeyed building in a classicist style reflects the imprint of several restorations. Most probably originally it consisted of two houses. In the past it had an arched baroque gateway, with a protruding balcony above it.

6 B **Piatsek House (Széchenyi tér 8.).** The baroque building dating from the beginning of the 18th century, was bought in 1816 by József Piatsek, a master builder of Pécs, and he rebuilt it in a classicist style. His grandson, Gyula Piatsek, completely rebuilt it in 1886: the result was a three storeyed eclectic building. After the liberation, the first "folk buffet" was opened on its groundfloor, later the Ibusz Travel Agency took over the premises both on the ground and first floors.

The memory of the former classicist style was preserved by the *segment arched gateway* and the *relief* in a classicist style above the entrance of the small shop next to the gate, as well as by the arcaded glass *facade* of the *courtyard wing*. After its restoration, the Pécs Art Centre moves into the *Elephant block*.

48

A symbol of Pécs: the Television Tower on the Misina peak

Varoni: A view of Pécs (mid-19th century. Lithograph)

The old town centre

Széchenyi square

A quiet courtyard on Széchenyi square

The Zsolnay fountain

The "Szerecsen" Pharmacy

"Elephant House" (Jókai square)

The southern line of houses on Jókai square

The University Library

Vasváry House (Kossuth Lajos utca 19.)

Neo-classic apartment house (Kossuth Lajos utca 61.)

The Synagogue (Kossuth tér 5.)

A house in romantic style in Sallai street

Houses in Sallai street, in front of them the Bath of Pasha Memi

Uitz Museum (Káptalan utca 4.)

Teachers' House (István tér 6.)

A statue of Janus Pannonius by Miklós Borsos in the Barbican garden

Relics from the Romanesque age (Stone collection)

Dóm square

Cathedral: part of the alabaster altar (17th century)

Interior of the Cathedral

Episcopal Palace: the staircase with Flemish gobelin

Baranya County Library (Geisler Eta street)

Baroque coat-of-arms above one of the entrances to the Library

Mosque of Pasha Hassan Jakovali at Rákóczi road

Flórián square

The Rókus Chapel in Alkotmány utca

The former Episcopal administrative building in Kulich Gyula utca

View from the tower of the Town Hall

The new town centre

May Day parade

A fine example of modern architecture:
the MÁV State Railways building on Lenin square

Bosnian houses in Ady Endre street

The Calvary

Várkonyi Nándor Library

The Paulite Church on Hunyadi road

Dwelling built into the mountainside

Old houses on the side of Havi-hegy

Chapel on Havi-hegy

View from behind an old house on Havi-hegy

Old roofs in Tettye valley

Felsőmalom utca 9.: the courtyard of the Timár House

7 B   **The former Pécs Savings Bank** (Széchenyi 9—
10.). A four level building from 1898 in eclectic
style. The two plots were originally the sites of the
Czyndery and Cséby Houses. During his sojourn in
Pécs, Emperor Josef II, later Hungarian King, stayed
in the Czyndery House in 1770. In 1950, the Baranya
County Council moved into the building. At present
it is used as an office building. Earlier, the Royal
Coffee-house was situated on its ground floor.

8 B   **"Asztalos János" Secondary School Students'
Hostel** (Széchenyi tér 11.). Originally built as
a Jesuit monastery, later it became the law academy.
For a long time, a military hospital and barracks operated in the building, finally a grammar school moved
in. Until the nationalisation, it was used as the Pécs
Chief Grammar School of the Cistercian order.

The puritan character of the building is emphasized
by the *pilaster strips* extending to the full height of
the structure, as well as the *ledges*. In the past, the
entrance was in the middle of the building and the
church was connected with the monastery by a corridor. This was demolished in 1864.

The Jesuits acquired the plot in 1689, which at the
end of the Turkish era belonged to Achmed Zaim.
Construction work went on from 1716 to 1720 and was
completed is 1724. The stones of the Turkish cemetery
of the Szigeti suburb were built into the walls. In
1849, the monastery and grammar school were turned
into a military hospital and in 1856 into barracks. Then
for the purpose of a guard post, an earthen terrace
was constructed in front of the building, which existed
until 1897.

The southern wing was built in 1864, with a small
turret over its house chapel. (After the nationalisation
of the schools, the turret was removed.) In 1935, a
new modern school was built, according to the designs
of Gyula Gosztonyi.

The temporary exhibition hall of the Pécs Gallery
was opened in the cellars of the Students' Hostel,
with an entrance from the Széchenyi Alley. Its exhibitions belong among the highest ranking artistic

events of Pécs. (Small sculpture and ceramic biennales.)

A *swimming pool* was opened on the courtyard of the school in 1947, its 33.3 m long open-air pool can be visited in the summer.

In 1958, a *Leonardo da Vinci bust* by György Baksa Soós was unveiled in front of the eastern facade of the new building.

9 B **The former Országh House** (Széchenyi tér 12.). The building, which was later called the Prandau House, is used today by the archeological department of the Janus Pannonius Museum. An archeological exhibition covering the history of Baranya from ancient times to the Árpád era is open to the public.

The first data about the house are known from 1687. According to the records, it belonged to Ibrahim Csór, then to the Jesuits, who set up a school in it. Later it was turned into a tavern, and between 1774 and 1782 it was possessed by the Országh family. In the 19th century, it went into the possession of the Prandau, then the Nádasy and later of the Visnya families. It was handed over for the purposes of the museum in 1950.

The single storeyed Baroque building with neo-classic elements, has a richly articulated facade with *middle projection and segment arched gateway*.

The back part of the building and the wing on Hunyadi út were built later.

10 B **2nd district wedding hall** (Széchenyi tér 13.). Earlier it was called the Eiser House. Its present form was given in the 1950s when the present Hunyadi (then: Stalin) road was widened, and half of the building was pulled down, and its southern entrance walled up. The neo-classic building lost considerably from its value with these transformations.

11 B **Baranya County Court** (Széchenyi tér 14.). The former Oertzen House was rebuilt in 1891 in an early eclectic style. Although an additional storey was added and the uniform ledge line of the eastern side of the square—developed in the 19th century—was somewhat disrupted, with its noble lines and well articulated facade, it belongs among the valuable buildings of the square.

The medieval bath, rebuilt by the Turks, was still extant here in 1695, in a rather dilapidated condition. The County used it as a prison in the 1720s and in 1780; as a permanent tax settlement of the County Hall, the County handed over the bath to the town, then in 1786 it was bought by judge Zsigmond Petrovszky. In 1804, the plot was bought by György Hegedüs, the Prefect of the Németboly estate. He pulled down the bath and replaced it with a two storey Baroque style building. From 1836 the Pécs Burghers' Casino operated in it.

On the eastern part of the estate, in Mária utca (today: Déryné street) the first stone theatre of Pécs was built in 1839, in which first German, later exclusively Hungarian companies performed. The building of the theatre, together with the house on Széchenyi square went into private hands. By the eighties, it was in such a poor condition that the authorities did not permit further performances. The last performance was held in 1886 in the theatre. In 1890, the reconstruction of the former Casino building started, together with the demolition of the run down theatre. In 1891, the building of the Royal Court was completed according to the designs of Imre Schlauch.

12 B **Nádor Hotel** (Széchenyi tér 15.). Originally this was the parish office. In 1845, the building was bought by the Schönherr family, and the hotel called the Nádor was built by 1846. The hotel had 30 rooms, and on its groundfloor a coffee-house. The hotel quickly became popular because of its good rooms and excellent cuisine. It catered for the most exacting guests, and was particularly popular among actors and actresses from the capital. Cornélia Prielle was a regular guest of the hotel. However, the hotel—built in a romantic style—proved to be too small for the increased clientele, therefore, the old building was pulled down in 1902 and a new hotel was built, again according to the designs of Imre Schlauch, with more rooms and more luxury. (The de luxe parlour furniture can be seen at the exhibition of the Catering Industrial Museum in Budapest.)

The *Nádor Söröző* (Beerhall) is famous, as well as the only "genuine" *coffee-house* of Hungary, a meeting point for the eminent personalities, artists, writers and scientists of Pécs and of Hungarian public life. The hotel complex also includes the *Mecsek Cukrászda* (cake shop) in the romantic building of No. 16.

13 B **The former Zsolnay House** (Széchenyi tér 17.). A three level romantic apartment house, built for the Zsolnay family in 1845, simultaneously with the buildings at No. 16 and 18. The editorial offices of Jelenkor (Present Age), the literary periodical of Pécs, occupy the first floor. In fact the building has two entrances, in the past the excellent Nick Beerhall could be found in the romantic glass roofed passage. Today, a quiet snack bar called the Finom falatok (Fine titbits) operates here.

14 B **Inner-city Church** (Széchenyi tér). In the Middle Ages, a large Gothic triple aisled church stood here, facing the east, with a polygonal sanctuary termination—the parish church called St. Bertalan. The northern part of the square was almost completely taken by the basilica and the churchyard around it. The second largest church of the town was pulled down by the Turks in the second half of the 16th century, and with the use of its stones they built the largest mosque in Hungary, the djami of Pasha Gazi Kassim. The mosque was built on a regular square ground plan in a cube shape with its "mihrab" directed towards Mecca. An octagonal, inside circular squat cupola covers the building. Originally a pillared entrance hall covered by three cupolas joined the north-western side. On the facade, on three levels ogee arched windows and lancet windows can be seen on the side of the drum.

The archeological exploration of the mosque was carried out by Gyula Gosztonyi between 1939 and 1942. When investigating the Baroque tower and the adjoining later additions, the base of the minaret was found in the north-western corner, together with the mihrab (prayer niche) and the remnants of the stalactite vault. This excavation brought up many fine carved stones of the medieval St. Bertalan Church.

After the expulsion of the Turks, the mosque was turned into the church of the Jesuits, who carried out numerous transformations. This was when the Turkish entrance hall disappeared, replaced by the cupola covered choir adjoined on both sides by a chapel and sacristy. The entrance was opened to the south. The minaret was pulled down in 1753, and replaced by a tower. Finally, a gallery was built on arcades, leading to the grammar school. The restorations were completed by the building of a neo-renaissance cupola at the beginning of our century.

On the basis of Nándor Körmendy's design, a semicircular part of the square was built around the former mosque During the restoration, the later additions were removed (the corridor was demolished somewhat earlier). As a late completion of the restorations, the original cupola was restored in the 1950s. The painting of the building was carried out by Ernő Gebauer, a well known painter of Pécs.

The church is the largest and finest relic of Turkish architecture in Hungary and even in its present form one of the most eminent creations of 16th century architecture.

15 B **Trinity statue** (Széchenyi tér). In 1713, the Town Council decided to erect the Trinity statue on the Main square. The first statue was the work of András Berchardt, a sculptor of Pécs. From that time on, the main square was called Trinity square for several decades. The second statue was completed in 1750, which then stood there for 150 years. The work of András Merchardt, a sculptor of Pécs, had deteriorated by the end of the past century.

György Kiss, a famous sculptor, born in Szászvár, was commissioned to make the third statue. The present Trinity statue was consecrated in 1908.

16 B **The mounted statue of János Hunyadi** (Széchenyi tér). The bronze statue stands on a

53

limestone pedestal and it was erected in the lower corner of the "upper" square in 1956 to commemorate the 500th anniversary of the Nándorfehérvár victory over the Turks in 1456. A competition preceded the erection of the statue, in which Pál Pátzay, József Somogyi and Ferenc Medgyesi also participated. The first prize was won by Pál Pátzay and he was commissioned to do the work. The location of the statue and the decision of the jury and other details provoked much dispute. Today, the waves have settled and the people have become accustomed to the strange place where the statue was erected.

17 B **Vilmos Zsolnay memorial fountain** (Széchenyi tér). The designer was Andor Pilch, its material: glazed pyrogranite, made in the Zsolnay Factory in 1912. Its present spot was selected in 1930, a small square in front of the Church of the Good Samaritans. The ox headed gargoyles of the fountain in an art nouveau style and the ornaments are decorated with eosin glaze. The model was a drinking vessel, part of the gold treasure found at Nagyszentmiklós. Since Turkish times, there was always a fountain on this square. During the expulsion of the Turks, these were demolished, but they were replaced—not far away—at the beginning of the 18th century by the town authorities. They were pulled down at the end of the century, but with replacement in mind. The fountain erected in 1930 was a gift of Miklós Zsolnay to the town.

The bronze *memorials* the "19th Pécs Infantry" by Ferenc Sidló on the eastern side of the balustraded interior square, and the "52nd Pécs Infantry" on the western side were unveiled in 1932. With this, homage was paid to the Pécs regiments of the First World War.

THE AREA AROUND SZÉCHENYI SQUARE

J ó k a i s q u a r e can be approached from two directions from Széchenyi square. Attentive observers may shake their heads: who has ever seen such a strangely shaped square! In fact it is not only a square, but also a street. The explanation can be found in the past. In fact the street broadens from Széchenyi square in a funnel-like manner, then to the north-east it ends in a small alley-like projection. Today the whole ensemble is called Jókai square.

Of course, in the past it was different. The square and the street had separate names. The street was called Schmidt Gasse (1722), Platea Fabrorum (1759), then (according to sources) "Street leading from the small market to the Cloister of the Capuchins" (1784). Thus it involves the street leading from the square to the monastery of the Good Samaritans, today to the No. 2 Clinic. The square had various names during the past 200 years: Alte Fleisch Markht, Alte Fisch-markht, Fischmarkt (1722), Kis tér, Kispiac, and since 1893 Jókai tér. According to the oldest names, this was the fish market in the 18th century (later the fish market was in the present Hal tér—Fish square), then the vendors ousted from the Nagypiac (Large market—present Széchenyi tér) settled here with their stalls, this explains the name Kispiac (Small market). Despite the earlier mentioned strange shape, it was always a closed square with an intimate atmosphere, with the narrow alley-like projection towards Jókai street (later this was broadened). It had a similar exit to the north-east, towards Széchenyi square and one is still astonished how the tram managed to get through here (since 1913). The exit towards Sallai street is also rather narrow.

Despite its strange and irregular shape, this is still the most united square of Pécs with the most pleasant atmosphere. One feels the most direct link with the town itself: the houses here are in a human proximity. Although their style varies, they radiate a uni-form, pleasant, genuine old Pécs aura. This is not spoilt even by the turreted eclectic corner house of Geisler Eta street, and the building of the former Savings Bank (later the County Hall), which also had little towers in the past, in fact they add to the at-mosphere, protectively towering over the square.

Both in the past and today, the square was one of the centres of trading life. The houses were occupied by craftsmen and merchants, their workshops and shops were also in the buildings, several of them were very well known in their period. No. 2 housed a pharmacy in 1712, there was a cake shop in No. 5, a bakery in No. 6, and a barber, later a chirurgeon (physician) in No. 7.

No. 6 had the most interesting story. In 1712 there was a bakery in the house, in 1759 the house was bought by a locksmith and in 1799 by Ferenc Schneckenberger. Since then—acording to Pécs customs—the house was named after him. At that time, the large hall of the building provided a venue for various drama companies. In 1834, the following advertisement appeared in the "Társalkodó" (Conversation): "Last night the Baky drama company played in the Schneckenberger Hall." Since 1844, the Piatsek family owned the building. This is where the "Elephant" grocery was opened in 1876. The elephant trade sign was only later taken over by the restaurant.

The history of No. 1 is no less interesting. In 1713 Simon Radnics, a goldsmith bought the plot with the ruined, burnt down building. In 1784, a merchant bought it, then Count László Esterházy from whom Count Schmidegg, the former owner bought it back, only to pass it on to János Jager, a merchant. In 1878, a school for merchant apprentices operated in the building.

In a strange manner, part of the Piatsek House in Széchenyi square also belongs to Jókai square, where No. 2, 4 and 6 on Jókai square bear the numbers of Sallai street.

18 B **Elephant block** (Jókai square). The name is of recent origin. It was given at the beginning of the reconstruction and since then the name struck to it. The block of buildings, which are to be reconstructed, will be the house of arts in Pécs.

The block consists of 5 buildings. Their style differs, nevertheless, they add a uniform skyline to the street, whether we observe it from Széchenyi square, from Sallai street or from the southern side of the square. The Piatsek House (Széchenyi tér 8.) was built in eclectic style, the one below it, No. 7 in a baroque,

Jókai square No. 2 in neo-classic and No. 4 a romantic style. No. 6 on Jókai square is the simplest building. The eponym "Elephant House" was built in neo-classic style. The irregular block closes streets (Sallai and Geisler Eta) and separates Jókai from Széchenyi square.

19 B **Zsolnay centenary memorial fountain** (Jókai tér). Based on the design of Antal Gazder, the glazed pyrogranite fountain was erected in 1968 on the 100th anniversary of the Zsolnay Factory.

Kossuth Lajos utca

The street enters the eastern side of Széchenyi square at the northern side of the Council Hall.

Presumably this was always the main street of Pécs. When after the Tartar invasion, the town was surrounded by walls, one of the most important gateways of the town was built at the end of this street. Trading in the town was carried out between the Budai and Szigeti gateways. The main square was the market, where the merchants arriving from the east or west displayed their goods. Most of them arrived through the high street. The Tettye brook flowed in front of the eastern town gateway, with mills along its banks, a bridge spanned the brook, and led to the gate through which the road continued into the town. It was lined on the right and left by small shops and workshops, where the best craftsmen and merchants of Pécs worked and lived.

The 1554 Turkish tax records mention it as Nagy utca (Big street). The listed names mostly defined crafts: 4 Mészáros (Butcher), 2 Szabó (Tailor), 1 Ötvös (Silversmith), 7 Varga (Cobbler), 1 Ács (Carpenter), 1 Szűcs (Furrier), 1 Kerékjártó (Wheelwright), 2 Kalmár (Merchant), and 1 Asztaljártó (Cabinet-maker) occurred in the list. According to the 1678 register the number of intact houses and hardly ruined buildings was surprisingly significant after the siege in Nagy utca. It recorded that several houses were in inhabitable condition. Obviously they remained here from the Middle

Ages, naturally they were not pulled down, but extended and reconstructed and perhaps they are still extant.

The main street of Pécs had various names over the past 300 years: initially as it was mentioned it was called Nagy utca, less frequently Öregh utca (Old street), then Fő utca (High street). Later it became Király utca (King street) and after 1945: Kossuth Lajos utca. When the town gates were pulled down (at the end of the 18th century), the road outside the walls organically joined the main street, but to the east of Sörház utca (Brewery street) it was named for a long time otherwise. In fact this part belonged to the Budai suburb. This was Kossuth Lajos utca.

The first houses were mostly two storeyed, with a workshop or small shop on the ground floor. On two major plots, two Turkish mosques stood in the High street. One was used by the Paulites to build a church and monastery (today: Széchenyi grammar school), the other by the Dominicans. After the dissolution of the orders, the Paulite monastery was taken over by the county and used as the County Hall, then various schools used it (Law Academy, grammar school, college, teachers' training school, and secondary school). The Dominican monastery was first turned into a military hospital, then into a military school. Later the church was turned into an apartment building. The monastery was pulled down at the end of the past century, a small square was set up and the Pécs National Theatre was built in the middle.

The monastery ensemble of the Dominicans was faced by a building surrounded by strong walls, the Treasury Salt Depot (today: the OTP Savings Bank and the Baranya County Archives). Beside it, the National Casino was opened in 1839 (today: the cultural centre of the garrison). Well-to-do Pécs burghers (Zsolnay, Nendtvich, Hamerli and Vasváry), noblemen of Baranya (Jeszenszky and Rihmer) and officers (Ottinger) owned houses in the High street. In the past, it indicated a status to reside here, the street was the centre of trade, culture and prosperity. Coffee-houses (Otthon), hotels (Aranyhajó, Magyar Király and Pannónia), and shops existed alongside each other. In 1913, trams were introduced in Pécs, first along the High street. With this, most of the traffic was concentrated here. Today, when a person in Pécs says: "I go to town"—he primarily refers to Kossuth street. Visitors to the town also do the same.

Színház tér (Theatre square) is an organic part of Kossuth Lajos utca, which was artificially developed in 1893 after pulling down the Dominican monastery and building the theatre. In fact no numbered house would belong to it if—ingeniously—the buildings lining the square from two sides would not have been given two numbers, one marking Kossuth Lajos street, the other Színház square and one (No. 3) Perczel street. Strangely enough the theatre was given only one number. Officially it is Kossuth Lajos utca 16, but logically although not quite regularly it uses Színház tér 1, with the argument that the building of the theatre belongs not only officially, but also organically to No. 1 since the connecting wing was built.

20 c **Kossuth Lajos utca 1.** A four storeyed romantic apartment house, connected with Széchenyi square through a glass-covered passage. The designs of the building were drawn up in Vienna on the order of Vilmos Zsolnay, and the house was completed in 1895. Above the broad middle window on the first floor, the inscription: "Bazár" can be seen.

21 c **Former "Arany Hajó"** (Kossuth Lajos utca 3.). In its present form, the (Golden Ship) guest house was built at the beginning of the 19th century in a neo-classic style.

22 c **Former Pannonia Hotel** (Kossuth Lajos utca 5.). The design of the building in art nouveau style was made by Andor Pilch in 1913. In the 18th century, two buildings owned by the Petrovszky family stood on the site of the hotel, which were united and rebuilt in 1799 by Zsigmond Petrovszky the Subprefect of the County. This was marked on the carved stone balcony: "Renovatum est Anno 1799". When the building was demolished, the balcony was presented

59

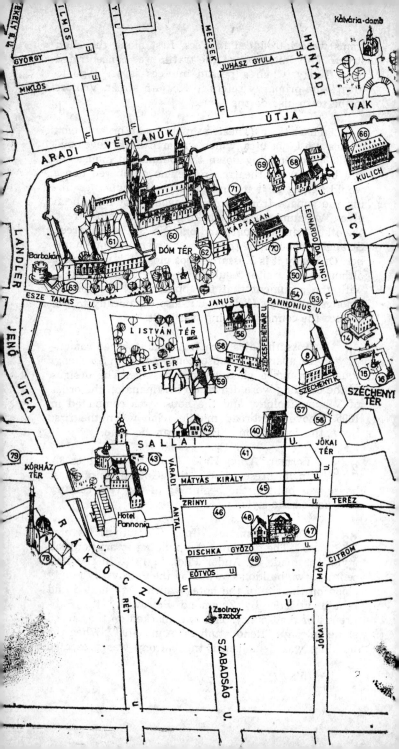

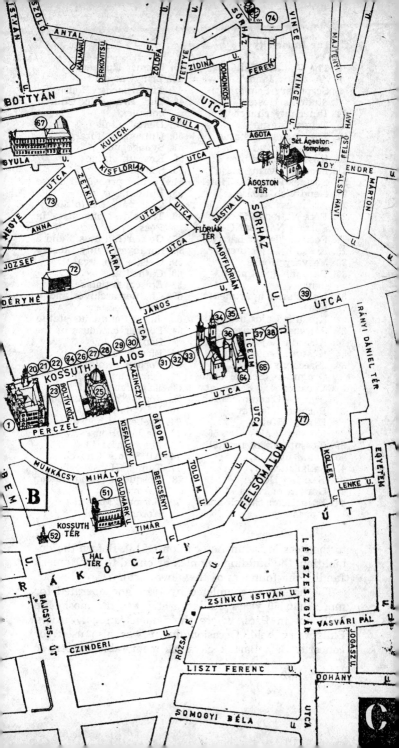

C The Inner-city

1. The Council Hall
8. "Asztalos János" Secondary School Students Hostel
14. Inner-city church
15. Trinity statue
16. The mounted statue of János Hunyadi
20. Kossuth Lajos utca 1.
21. Former "Arany Hajó"
22. Former Pannonia Hotel
23. Nendtvich House
24. Archives
25. Pécs National Theatre
26. Former National Casino
27. Former "Fehér hattyú"
28. Kossuth Lajos utca 17.
29. Vasváry House
30. Baroque apartment house
31. Neo-classic apartment house
32. Kossuth Lajos utca 32.
33. Jeszenszky House
34. Kossuth Lajos utca 41.
35. Kossuth Lajos utca 43.
36. "Széchenyi István" Grammar School and Vocational Secondary School—Liceum church
37. Former "Magyar Király" Hotel
38. Kossuth Lajos utca 50.
39. Kossuth Lajos utca 61.
40. Sallai utca 14.
41. Sallai utca 21.
42. Kóczián House
43. Garden of ruins
44. Franciscan church and monastery
45. Former Nunnery
46. Zrínyi utca 13.
47. Mitterpacher House
48. The Evangelic Church complex
49. Dental clinic
50. University library
51. Synagogue
52. Kossuth statue
53. School
54. Former prebendal house
55. Building of the Csontváry Exhibition
56. The oldest pharmacy in Pécs
57. Geisler Eta utca 3 and 5
58. Baranya County Library
59. Geisler Eta utca 21.
60. Cathedral
61. Episcopal palace
62. Chapter archives and parish rectory
63. Janus Pannonius statue
64. Former outhouse of the Paulites
65. Liceum utca 7.
66. Former seminary
67. Old County Hall
68. Káptalan utca 2.
69. Former prebendal house
70. Káptalan utca 5.
71. Prebendal house
72. Majláth House
73. Megye utca 18.
74. All Saints' Church
77. Tanner House
78. Mosque of Pasha Hassan Jakovali
79. Former "Magyar Korona" Hotel

to the Pécs Museum Association (1913). Before the demolition, the building complex belonged to the Hamerli family, the founders of the glove factory.

The hotel was completed by 1915, and operated for more than 60 years. Its large hall was the most elite ballroom in Pécs, where the famous annual Jurists' Balls were held. Occasionally, it was also used for concerts. Béla Bartók gave his memorable concert in this hall in 1929. After the liberation, in the 1950s it was used for a time as a chamber theatre, later as a night club. The Pannonia Cellar was also a well known restaurant and place of entertainment. The hotel was closed in the 1970s and for more than 15 years now it has been waiting for renovation.

23 c **Nendtvich House** (Kossuth Lajos utca 8.). A two level romantic style building. The framing of the richly decorated window openings were made from glazed ceramics. In fact this is characteristic of most houses in Pécs built in a romantic style. And this is no coincidence, because the construction tallied with the first prosperity of the Zsolnay Factory in Pécs. The ceramic ornaments were manufactured in the factory. The well-to-do burghers of Pécs quickly became fond of it and richly employed this type of decoration on their buildings. This house was owned by the Nendtvich family, who gave eminent personalities to the town, ranging from a chemist to the mayor of the town. Károly Nendtvich also lived here, the famous Hungarian chemist and natural scientist, the eponym of a rare plant of the Mecsek (Doronicum Nendtvich). A *memorial plaque* was placed on the wall of the building on December 19, 1909 to commemorate his work.

24 c **Archives** (Kossuth Lajos utca 11.). After the expulsion of the Turks, this area belonged to the Treasury, and in 1695 this was also the State Treasury. From the north, the present Archives are still surrounded by a several hundred year-old castle-like fence, which in its time protected the Salt Depot of the Treasury. The present building was constructed in 1872 utilizing one or two walls of the former Salt Depot. The earlier two storeyed Baroque facade was replaced by a three storeyed building in period style.

The financial authorities handed over the building in 1950 and it became the complex of the Baranya County Archives. It is the country's largest provincial archives, although its historic material only dates back to the expulsion of the Turks. In addition to the rich material of the former county and urban archives, researchers can

63

work with a large collection of court, land register, estates and rural documents. The vast *collection of maps* is of special value, the *cartulary* and the highly valuable single collections, among which the letters patent of the town of Pécs from 1780 are the best known. The archives also preserve considerable *material* concerning the *working class movement* of Baranya and Pécs.

Since the seventies, the Archives became the genuine workshop for local history research. The institution publishes historic works of national significance.

25 c   **Pécs National Theatre** (Kossuth Lajos 16—Színház tér 1). Built between 1893—1895 in neo-renaissance style according to the designs of Antal Lang and Antal Steinhardt. During Turkish times, the plot together with the surrounding area—ranging from the present Boltiv köz to Kazinczy utca—belonged to the Turkish mosque and cemetery. In 1688, the Dominicans took it over. The monastery was consecrated in 1729—1930 and the church in 1771. In 1786, the order was dissolved and since 1809 the monastery was used as a military hospital, then as a military academy. After 1852 it was again a military hospital, then a poor-house, and in 1892 it was an isolation hospital.

The church belonging to the monastery was turned into an apartment house in 1835, and is still used for the same purpose (Kossuth Lajos utca 18. or Színház tér 2.).

The first stone theatre of Pécs—in present Déryné utca —was closed down by the authorities at the end of the past century. The companies played in the temporary wooden summer theatre in Dischka Győző utca. The plot for the new theatre was defined on the site of the Dominican monastery. The monastery was pulled down in 1893. The theatre was festively opened on October 5, 1895 and since then it became a centre of Pécs' cultural life. It was immediately opened after the liberation. On December 18, 1944 the parties which gathered in the Hungarian National Independence Front held a mass meeting in the theatre and elected their delegates to the National Assembly.

With its programme policy and company of excellent artists, the theatre became one of the significant theatres of the country from the 1950s onward, It has a drama and opera company, and a ballet corps. Since 1981, the Bóbita Puppet Ensemble—as an independent puppet theatre—has become a structural part of the Pécs National Theatre. The theatre and the Chamber Theatre, which operates in the former Trade Union Headquarters, have been connected through a wing built at the beginning of the 1970s.

The *Genius statue* standing on the main cupola and made of gilded tin by György Kiss, excels from among the rich decorations of the building. The others, the *female trio* above the tympanon, the *allegoric relief* on the tympanon, the *reliefs* depicting Mihály Vörösmarty, Ferenc Erkel, Gergely Csiky, Ede Szigligeti and Károly Kisfaludy and the *two* allegoric *female figures* were made of pyrogranite in the Zsolnay Factory.

26 c **Former National Casino** (Kossuth Lajos utca 13.). The predecessor of the house was most probably a Baroque building built between 1712 and 1722. In 1806, it was the home of Ferenc Ranolder, a glove-maker, and this is where János Ranolder, later Bishop of Veszprém was born. During its 1839 reconstruction, the facade was built in neo-classic style and the National Casino moved in. In 1894 it was pulled down. The new building of the National Casino was built in 1895. The original designs were made by Ágoston Kirstein, but because their accomplishment seemed to be too expensive, Imre Schlauch—the builder—revised them. After the liberation in 1945, the "Doktor Sándor" Cultural Centre operated in the building, then it was handed over to the Army Club. At the beginning of the 1970s, it was rebuilt and modernized. Nevertheless, its eclectic facade was left in its original form. Today, the Pécs Garrison Club of the Armed Forces uses the building.

At some period, the building was connected with the neighbouring Fehér hattyú (White Swan) guest house.

27 c **Former "Fehér hattyú"** (Kossuth Lajos utca 15.). Originally a Turkish building stood on the site. The present two storey building dates back to the beginning of the 19th century, this was turned into the "Fehér hattyú" guest house. Its large hall was the venue of reputed balls and concerts. In 1846, *Ferenc Liszt* gave a concert here and donated the income (350 forints) to the building of the chapel in the Budai suburb cemetery. The chapel—in romantic style—built according to the design of Ferenc Windisch, was pulled down in 1981.

28 c   **Kossuth Lajos utca 17.** The frequently reconstructed, neo-classic, later Baroque building, most probably dates back to the Middle Ages. In 1695, it was the residence of the military commanders of the town. At that time it was a two storey building. It survived the siege of the town intact. From later times, there is only recorded data about the building of the courtyard wing.

29 c   **Vasváry House** (Kossuth Lajos utca 19.). An apartment house in early eclectic style, the date of the building is unknown. Obviously it is the result of the transformation of an earlier (perhaps Baroque) building from the 1870s or 1880s. It was owned by the Treiber family, who changed their name to the Hungarian soundling Vasváry in 1883. The family's hardware shop was on the groundfloor.

It is a two storey building with a single axial *middle projection*. Its facade is articulated with a *stringcourse* and closed by a triple *main cornice*. Above it, an *attic* with balustrade that had 4 vases on its postaments. The middle phase is solid with the inscription: "Vasváry ház", above it an allegoric *female figure* with the coat-of-arms of the Vasváry family. Between the far end windows, rich relief decoration can be seen. The allegoric figures and the *stucco decoration* between the windows were made of pyrogranite in the Zsolnay Factory, and put up on the facade in 1897.

The courtyard of the house has a pleasant atmosphere, where the *allegoric group of statues* is repeated on the back facade.

The triple-windowed large middle *saloon* on the first floor, its early period furniture, wallpaper and fireplace are protected examples of applied art.

The *Memorial Room of Lajos Magyar,* a well known left-wing journalist of Pécs origin and an exhibition illustrating Pécs' rich musical life will be arranged in this building.

30 c   **Baroque apartment house** (Kossuth Lajos utca 21.). The building date of the two storey house is unknown. It is an early, perhaps medieval building, which was reconstructed on several occasions. The first data are from 1695, when a two storeyed and a single storeyed building stood on the plot. The former Baroque arched *gateway* is used as a shop window today.

31 c   **Neo-classic apartment house** (Kossuth Lajos utca 22.). A two storey building. Its eclectic facade was the result of a renovation at the end of the past century. The house was built earlier, perhaps at the beginning of the 19th century. Originally it was in neo-classic style. This is indicated by the *doorway*, the *iron gate* of the *staircase*, the *bannisters* and the *iron railing* of the courtyard corridor. The iron work allows us to presume that this may have been one of the finest neo-classic apartment houses of Pécs.

In the courtyard, the north-western wall of Pasha Ferhat's mosque can be seen, with the former walled up entrance.

32 c   **Kossuth Lajos utca 32.** A two storey apartment house, its facade in a romantic style was the result of a reconstruction around 1862, which involved the entire street wing. The building itself dates back much further. It was already marked as a two storeyed house in the 1695 records, thus it can be presumed that it was built in the Middle Ages.

Ágoston Sziberan opened his cake shop in the house in 1789. The cake shop is still extant. *János Paitler* was one of the famous coffee brewers, whose son, *Antal*, later Bishop of Vác, was also born here. The present Éva espresso bar is still mentioned—not officially—as the "Caflisch patisserie" after its former name.

33 c   **Jeszenszky House** (Kossuth Lajos utca 36.). A two storeyed Baroque apartment building, which dates back to the mid-18th century. The house was already there in 1777. However, the building has an earlier core, originating from 1695. Most probably the part to the east of the entrance was built at that time. In 1727, the western part was also joined to the plot. At that time, it belonged to Sub-prefect Dániel Horváth, whose daughter was married to János Jeszenszky. From that time on, it was called the Jeszenszky House. In 1796, Emánuel Jeszenszky added a decorative *wrought iron gate* to the bottom of the staircase with the monograms JE and FB (his own and his wife's). The coat-of-arms of the family was above the entrance, but today it is hardly visible. The building was reconstructed and renovated on several occasions, and it is still not restored in its original form.

The intersecting vaulted *gateway* is noteworthy, together iwth the *staircase* with the wrought iron gate, the baroque *bannister* and the *ballustrade* with tracery on the first floor. Similar tracery can be seen on the originally open, then walled up balcony.

34 c **Kossuth Lajos utca 41.** A two storeyed heptaaxial baroque apartment house. In the small niche between the third and fourth axis, the *statue of St. Dominic* made from limestone can be seen. The statue dates back to the 19th century, thus being younger than the building, which developed in its present form in the second half of the 18th century. Its core, a small single storeyed house already stood here in 1695 and was built in the Middle Ages.

The building is extremely puritan. A typical example of the Pécs burghers' houses. The only ornament (in addition to the statue which was added later) is the *ribbon framed decoration of the windows,* and the double axial slight *middle projection.* The seventh window axis may have been built later.

35 c **Kossuth Lajos utca 43.** The two storeyed completely characterless apartment house, built on four axes, has two interesting features, the *two small vaulted shops,* which already existed in 1695. Most probably the first floor and the courtyard annex were added to the small house of medieval origin in a later period. According to local traditions, a small coffee-house existed here in Turkish times.

36 c **"Széchenyi István" Grammar School and Vocational Secondary School—Liceum Church**

(Kossuth Lajos utca 44.). The area and the building have a lively history. According to some unconfirmed presumptions, this was the site in the Middle Ages of the Erzsébet Ispotály (Elizabeth Hospital). The mosque of Elhaji Hussein was built in 1619, during Turkish rule, somewhat nearer than the north-east corner of the plot. This small building survived the liberation struggles against the Turks—completely intact. Then the mosque was handed over to the Greek Orthodox denomination of Pécs for use as their church. However, they did not own it for a long time, because the Bishop of Pécs tried to persuade them to merge with the Roman Catholics, and as they refused, they were settled in 1693 on the site of present Rácváros. The former mosque stood empty for some time. In 1695, the newly settled Paulite Order took it over, but de jure they only acquired it in 1698 together with the ground on which it stood. During the 1704 so-called "Rác" devastation, the church and the small monastery, which stood on the same plot—burnt down. With the arrival of more peaceful times, the buildings were restored from the ruins. The construction of the church started in 1741, and it was consecrated in 1756. A year later, in 1757, the building of the new monastery commenced and it was completed in 1760. After the festive opening, the mosque was pulled down in the 1760s and the old monastery in 1766. The extension of the new monastery started in 1768, when the eastern wing was built. In 1779, the spires of the church were also completed. Most probably this is when the late-Baroque gateways were fitted in. The church and the monastery were built in a baroque style, according to the design of Máté Vépi, a Paulite monk of Nagyszombat origin.

Signs of the baroque and later neo-classic baroque style can equally be recognized on the facade of the church. The baroque monastery is constructed in a moderate manner. Its facade to the courtyard is very simple. The only decoration of the hardly articulated facade is the triple axial *middle projection*. The finest part of the building is the wrought iron baroque *gateway*, decorated with the Paulite coat-of-arms at the entrance to the staircase area. Its model was the gateway of the Paulite monastery near the Roman Porta Pia.

The church was only used for a few years by the Paulite brothers, because Joseph II dissolved the order in 1786. From that time onward, the building and church were used for various purposes. For some time, the monastery was an apartment building, and in 1809 a military hospital. The church was used as a store. At the end of the 18th century, theatre performances were held in the building. In 1818, the county bought the complex, together with the farmstead to the south of the estate. According to plans it should have been turned into the County Hall. The plans for the rebuilding were completed, according to these the church would have become the County Prison. Obviously this was the reason why Bishop Szepesy intervened in 1832 and bought all three buildings (the former monastery, church and farmstead) for the purpose of setting up a high school. The church was restored and again consecrated. The training of teachers started in the building in 1832 and in 1835 the high school (Liceum) was set up with the law school and teachers' training school. Tuition was suspended between 1849 and 1865, when the cistercian grammar school moved into the building, from 1856 it was a teachers' training school and from 1865 again the law academy used the building. Between 1872 and 1887, the buildings were restored. The church was painted by Xavér Ferenc Mücke, a well known painter. In 1922, a secondary school moved into the building. In the 1920s, the church was again renovated and the carved stone frame of the former entrance to the monastery was replaced. After the liberation in 1945, a teachers' training school operated in the building for some time and then the "Széchenyi István" Grammar School moved in. In the meantime, the shops on the groundfloor were removed and the building was restored with its original facade.

37 c   **Former "Magyar Király" Hotel** (Kossuth Lajos utca 48 or Felsőház utca 2). The two storey eclectic building was the headquarters of the opposition in the Reform Age, led by Kázmér Batthyány. During his single visit to Pécs in 1846, *Lajos Kossuth* resided here.

38 c **Kossuth Lajos utca 50.** A two storey building, the groundfloor in neo-classic and the first floor in romantic style. The *decorations* of the hood moulding above the two far windows on the first floor are attractive, as well as the double axial slight middle projection to Kossuth Lajos utca, and the dense line of *cantilevers* under the ledge. Together with the corner building of Sörház utca 1 built in romantic style, the two opposite houses provide a fine complex.

39 c **Kossuth Lajos utca 61.** A two storey apartment house in classicist style, which deeply protrudes towards the the courtyard in an "L" shape, with three axes on its street facade. A protruding *parapet* stretches along the first floor at the height of the breast work. The *hood moulding* extending along the groundfloor turns into an arch above the windows. All this and the arched *gateway* and the horizontal rustication of the groundfloor wall surface—show a close kinship with the building of the university library, which was designed by József Piatsek. Possibly he contributed to the reconstruction two years after the building of the library. The date: 1832 and the monogram of the builder, Erreth can be seen on the fine wrought iron banister of the straircase. The master builder reconstructed the former episcopal rest house for the Erreth family, the owners of the tannery.

Sallai utca

To the west of Széchenyi square, towards the former Szigeti Gate, the road leads via Sallai utca. This was one of the most important streets of Pécs, carrying the east-west transit traffic. Primarily due to this, it was always inhabited by craftsmen and merchants, who also had their workshops and shops here.

The name of the street frequently changed. We do not know its medieval name. At the beginning of the Turkish occupation—according to the tax records (def-ters)—there was a St. Ferenc (St. Francis) street in Pécs. Obviously, this must have been it, because the Franciscans already had their monastery here. In 1687, its name was Szigeti kapu utca, then in chronological order the following names appeared in archive sources: Szigether Strasse (1712), Franciscaner Gasse, Plateau Francicanorum, Barátok utcája (1804), A Szigeti-kapura vezető utca, Barát utca, Ferencziek utcája (from 1864), and Sallai utca (1950).

Most of the houses were presumably built over medieval foundations. Their majority reflect a baroque style, naturally with later transformations and reconstructions. After Váradly Antal utca, the street suddenly broadens and in front of the eastern facade of the church, it forms a small square, which narrows at the tower, then broadens again, through which the narrow intimate street suddenly becomes spacious and sunny. At every step it shows a new face. Since 1981, it has been a pedestrian precinct, new lights were installed and the old buildings have an attractive emphasis when lit up in the evening.

The tenants of the Sallai street houses were craftsmen and merchants, members of the old Pécs families. It is worthwhile to observe the houses No. 1 to 20 (from 1700 to 1900). No. *1* was occupied by a blacksmith and a baker, No. *3* by a bricklayer, plumber and merchant, No. *4* by a butcher and merchants (the famous Reéh family), No. *5* by a locksmith, tailor, cartwright and soaper, No. *6* by a butcher, cartwright and a saddler, No. *7* by a glazier, and potter, No. *8.* by a baker (between 1877—1882 a coffee-house called ''Kávé forrás'' operated here), No. *9* by a locksmith, the episcopal cooper, glazier, tailor and a merchant, No. *10* by a baker, No. *11* by a glazier, butcher and furrier, No. *12* by a cooper, hooper, lawyer, physician, surgeon and a merchant, No. *13* by a shoe-maker and a cooper, No. *14* by a another shoe-maker and cooper, No. *14* by a potter, No. *15* by a book-binder, No. *16* by a merchant and a tailor, No. *17* by a shoe-maker, cooper, book-binder, goldsmith and plumber, No. *18* by a cooper's assistant, merchant, German tailor, German boot maker, and a confectioner, No. *19* by a locksmith, soaper, tailor, organist and a gunsmith, and No. *20* by an organist, merchant, painter, furrier and a physician.

According to the latest list of protected art monuments, there are 4 art monument houses in the street, there are 11 of art monument character and 5 buildings, which are significant from the viewpoint of the town's appearance.

40 c   **Sallai utca 14.** A three storeyed apartment house, built in romantic style in 1861. It towers over the surrounding houses in an unusual manner, it oppresses its neighbours. Nevertheless, it is one of the finest examples of romantic architecture in Pécs. The extremely fine latticed building with its glazed, protruding balcony and harmonious proportions is of outstanding significance in the street. Its *gateway* and *staircase* with the wrought iron banister is particularly noteworthy. There are 2 two storeyed *pavilions,* built in a romantic style in the back courtyard, and a rather dilapidated, but finely carved baroque stone *fountain basin.*

In the mid-1860s, a nursery of *József Szigriszt,* operated in this building.

41 c   **Sallai utca 21.** A two storeyed neo-classic Baroque apartment building. Presumably it was not built at the same time. The core of the building, from the beginning of the 18th century, was situated to the east of the entrance, perpendicularly to the street. The house was already extant in 1712. The arcaded courtyard wing must have been built somewhat later. In the second half of the century, another building was erected on the western part of the plot, connected with the previous one on the second floor. Thus, an apartment house parallel with the street took shape, with a large baroque gateway in the middle. The niche in Louis XVI style, with the statue of *Florian,* the patron saint of Pécs, was completed in the last phase of the construction work. As the result of the work in phases, the entrance in not in the middle of the building, but the niche is. Consequently the building in asymmetric.

The floor, which was built later and simultaneously

73

is much more uniform. The facade above the separating ledge is divided into broad panels by pilaster strips, within which there are *coupled windows,* with framed hood mouldings. The wooden portico in the courtyard area above the entrance is of later origin and lends a particular atmosphere to the building.

42 c **Kóczián House (Sallai utca 24.).** A characteristic example of Pécs architecture, the two side facades turn towards the street, which means that two buildings were built at right-angles to the street. The two storeyed baroque house with its arched freely standing gateway and a small single storeyed house beside it, were already standing here in 1777. All this was characteristic of Pécs architecture. The next phase of the construction work would have been the building of the perpendicular floor to the street, namely, the connection of the two separate houses. But this was omitted.

The building is significant, because it was the home of *Sándor Kóczián* between 1850 and 1870, a talented poet of Pécs of a tragic fate. A *memorial plaque* on the wall explains this.

43 c **Garden of Ruins** (in front of Sallai utca 33.). In the past, this was the bath of Pasha Memi, its ruins were pulled down around 1880. Excavations were started at the end of the 1970s. The findings were conserved and restored with art monumental replacements.

44 c **Franciscan church and monastery** (Sallai utca). According to sources, the Franciscan monastery in Pécs was set up by the Korodi family in 1301. After occupying the town, the Turks turned the church—whose choir was at the eastern part according to the customs of the Middle Ages—into a mosque. The Gothic choir may have been pulled down at the same time. In 1687, General János Thüngen handed the church back to the returned Franciscans, but they only received the monastery in 1721. Until 1727, the Franciscans reconstructed the church on several occasions. The western choir and the sanctuary were

built last. In the 1730s, the monastery was extended.
In 1738, a pharmacy was also opened, moreover, a felt
workshop was also set up in the southern wing of the
monastery. The building of the tower started in 1745.
The Franciscan brothers continuously built and extended their monastery and church, even in the 20th
century, until the order ceased to operate in Pécs.

The characteristically baroque helm roof of the
church was added in 1807, according to the design of
Mathias Fölsinger, an eminent architect of Pécs. It is
built on a single naved ground plan, with a line of
chapels on its northern side, and an ambulatory choir.
Its facade is in eclectic style, but the two floors of the
tower and the helm have remained unchanged, as indicated by the extant design of Fölsinger.

Its interior is fine baroque work, most probably done
by Franciscan brothers. The inlaid baroque *line of cabi-
nets* in the choir is of outstanding beauty, the handiwork
of Brother Lukács Jani from 1745.

The *monastery* is a two storey baroque building
without any decoration, but its mass—from the south—
makes a good impression. The facade in Sallai utca is
single storeyed, because of the rising ground. The bas-
ket railings of the windows were made in 1768, formerly decorating the windows of the cathedral chapter
house.

Jókai Mór utca and its side streets

Jókai Mór utca opens from Jókai tér in a southern
direction. After the expulsion of the Turks, this was
the residence of the Treasury Provisor, therefore, for
decades it was called Provisorata Gasse. At that time,
it was a cul de sac, because it ended at the Gardens
in front of the Town Hall. The town wall was only
broken through much later in 1885, and the road was
opened towards the Ország útja (today: Rákóczi út).

To the south, the street ends in a small square—at
the present building of the Post Office—which in fact
consisted of the funnel-like extending mouth of Citrom utca (Lemon street). The expiscopal ornamental
gardens were situated to the west and south—towards

the town wall [this explains the later name of the neighbouring street: Kert utca (Garden street) today: Dischka Győző utca].

Jókai Mór utca was lined by single and two storeyed buildings. The Treasury Provisor lived in a two storeyed house (Jókai utca 8). This plot was later taken over by the bishop, with the lodges of the episcopal gardener and cooper. Obviously it was no coincidence that a cartwright and a wheelwright, a carpenter, a cooper and a hooper lived in this street in the 18th century. The church and monastery of the Benedictines stood in the mouth of Citrom utca in the Middle Ages. Its high ruins were still extant after the Turks. A stone mason and bricklayer settled in its neighbourhood, and started to dismantle the ruins with the permit of the town, naturally using the material in other building work. Finally, almost nothing remained of the walls of the former Gothic church. In the 19th century, the Kindergarten (nursery) of the Women's Association, led by József Szigriszt, operated here on the site of the present Post Office. Theatre director, Károly Somogyi and carpenter Kléber built the wooden summer theatre in its back courtyard on an empty spot, which seated 1,200 spectators and where highly successful performances were held for many years in the absence of a permanent theatre.

In fact, Jókai Mór utca was a side street, and only acquired significance at the beginning of the 20th century, when the Post Office was constructed between 1902 and 1904. At that time, it became a genuine street with an exit to Rákóczi út. In the first half of the century, it was named Deák Ferenc utca, then in 1954 Jókai Mór utca, and a few years later, after the Franz Joseph I Turkish Baths were demolished, a new street —built to the south of Rákóczi út was also linked with it, thus lengthening it to the railway station.

Today, Jókai utca starts out from the old town centre, passes through the new town centre, linking the past with the present. The street and its neighbourhood are one of the oldest residential areas of the inner-city.

Most of the houses in the zig-zagging T e r é z   u t c a opening to the left, were built in the 18th and 19th centuries. The street already appeared on the 1687 Haüy map, together with present Mátyás király, Zrínyi and Dischka Győző streets.

The first name of Mátyás király utca can be found in the 1722 land register under the name: Obere Franciscaner Gasse. Between 1804 and 1864, it was called: Apácza utca (Nun street) hinting at the nunnery in the street. In 1864, the name was changed to Hunyadi utca, and in 1948 to Mátyás király utca.

45 c **Former Nunnery** (Mátyás király utca 15.). Most probably built in 1776 as indicated by the date in the Klimó coat-of-arms above the entrance. However, it may be that the date indicates a reconstruction and the building has an earlier history. In fact the Franciscan nuns moved in here in 1768. Their building must have been much smaller. Until 1856, a girls' school operated in the building and for one year it was used as a military prison. In 1857, a secondary school moved in. When the secondary school became a high school in 1870, the shortage of room became so acute that in 1881 the building was completely rebuilt and a floor added to the nunnery.

Béla Vikár and *János Kodolányi* were students of the secondary school. Today the *Ferenc Liszt Academy of Music* uses the building.

46 c **Zrínyi utca 13.** The modern history of the house is significant, although the building is very old. According to sources it already existed in 1722. The eastern facade clearly reflects baroque signs. In the 18th century, it must have been the characteristic house of a prosperous Pécs burgher. In the past century, it was transformed on several occasions and a new eclectic facade added. The building was the centre of the Pécs working class movement for 40 years. Between 1905 and 1945, it was the headquarters of the Pécs Organisation of the Hungarian Social Democratic Party, the Workers' Home and the centre of the trade union committee. All this is recorded by a plaque on the wall of the building.

The eponym of D i s c h k a   G y ő z ő   u t c a was the former scholar and extremely popular headmaster of the High School. Before 1912, it was called Kert utca, before that Aloe utca, Seiler Stadt. Prior to 1687, it was called Dervis bég utca. The first among the historic art monument buildings of present Dischka Győző utca in No. 8, a house in romantic style. The house with a decorative gable towards the street, was built around 1865, replacing a building which was already there in 1695.

47 c **Mitterpacher House** (Dischka Győző utca 2.). The oldest building in the street. From 1825 onwards it was an orphanage. Originally it belonged to Ignác Mitterpacher, an administrator of Pécsvárad, who built it in 1744. The originally baroque building was rebuilt at the beginning of the 19th century in neo-classic style.

48 c **The Evangelic Church complex** (Dischka Győző utca 4—6.). Adjoining the two sides of the church, are the *rectory* and the *ministry* built in 1875 in a romantic style. The *altar piece* of the church was painted by Viktor Madarász.

49 c **Dental Clinic** (Dischka Győző utca 5.). Built in 1873, for the purposes of an urban gymnasium. The foundation stone was laid by Count György Majláth, the last Lord Chief Justice. In its own time, this was the most modern and most attractive, best equipped gymnasium in the country. It was the venue of highly successful gymnastic tournaments. At the turn of the century and until the First World War, significant meetings were held by the workers at the sports ground next to the hall. The summer theatre was also built beside the hall. In 1888, the first Pécs industrial fair was held on the site.

Earlier, the Anatomy Institute of the University was here.

Leonardo da Vinci utca

Leonardo da Vinci utca opens from Széchenyi square in a northern direction. It is the finest and most uniform, perhaps even one of the oldest streets of Pécs. There was a street here already in the Middle Ages. It is also marked on the well known map of Josef Haüy from 1687. Beside the building in the middle of the street (most probably of medieval origin) there is an arched stone framed *gateway,* one of the four gates of Pécs which were provably built in the Middle Ages; two similar gates can be seen at the entrance to Káptalan utca 2.

At the beginning of the last century, the street towards the main square was narrow in an alley-like manner. On the corner the building of the former Jesuit school, and the later normal school of medieval origin could be seen. This was pulled down in 1882 and replaced by the present school building. On the other side, the plot of Countess Prandau was to be found. In 1830, Bishop Szepesy commissioned József Piatsek to build the episcopal college, which from 1832 provided a permanent home for the famous Klimó Library. (Today: it is the University library.) A narrow alley led to the library. The street had to be broadened, but the owner of the garden was unwilling to give up any of the ground. Finally, the town appropriated the necessary area, and succeeded in widening the street. The development of the northern part of the street is linked with the name of József Piatsek. He planned and built the prebendal house (Káptalan utca 3) on the north-western corner and with this and the connecting fence, developed the final form of the western side of the street.

The old definitions of Leonardo da Vinci street were connected with the school: in 1722 it was called Schuller Gässl, in 1804 Oskola utca, Schul Glasse, and in 1843 Kis oskola utca. In 1864 it became Szepesy utca, and in 1953 it was renamed Leonardo da Vinci street.

The present view of the street developed by the end of the past century. Opposite the library there were *two* single storey *buildings* in *romantic style.* To the south, on the north-east corner of the street there was a two storey eclectic house in 1889 and the same year the two storeyed building of the cathedral music school was also completed.

The buildings of the street are excellent examples of the harmonious unity of various styles. The classicist facade of the library excels with its particular beauty from the garland of the noble line of modest buildings. From the north, the street is closed by Káptalan utca 2. and from the south the line of houses on the western side of Széchenyi square.

50 c **University library** (Leonardo de Vinci utca 3.). It was built in 1830 in classicist style, based on the design of József Piatsek. Originally, Bishop Ignác Szepesy intended the building to be a college and the humanities faculty was festively opened in the new building in 1831. However, when the former Paulite monastery became available, the college moved into the High street building (Kossuth Lajos utca) and the new college building became free. The bishop used it for the famous *"Klimó collection"*, the library.

It is a two storey building. The first floor is separated by a strongly protruding *string course* and a triple extending *main cornice* closes it. The *portal* is held by four Toscanian engaged columns, extending to both floors. They support a triangle main cornice decorated with protruding large cantilevers. Between the engaged columns, the gateways and the windows on the groundfloor are semicircular. On the groundfloor the facade is horizontally rusticated. A *transom* runs along above the unframed windows, going into an arch above the windows. The *windows on the first floor* are square ended and ribbon framed, and there are recessed *mirrors* above the windows between the engaged columns.

In the twenties and thirties, a fierce dispute broke out behind closed doors about the building of the library, the number one art monument of Pécs, which stood in an unworthy surrounding, closed in a narrow alleyway. Therefore, the qualities of the building did not appear to the view. However, if the opposite buildings were pulled down, then through the then Inczédy

Dénes utca, with other demolitions towards Megye utca, an impressive square could be opened up, and the building would then have a "worthy" milieu. The dispute was settled by the ecconomic situation—there was no money for the demolition work. With this, four historic art monuments were saved from demolition, although—on a study level—the reconstruction designs by Gyula Gosztonyi were already complete. Fortunately, they remained unaccomplished.

In fact architect József Piatsek consciously designed the college building into a narrow street. Exactly because of the narrow street, he designed engaged columns for the portal, which ensured that from the narrow street, from both directions and from the opposite side, the building is enjoyable and visible.

The famous *library*, founded by György Klimó in 1774, was settled in the building in 1832—1836, according to the instructions of Bishop Ignác Szepesy: "The library housed in the espiscopal palace has to be resettled in the two rooms, where earlier philosophy lectures were held and it has to be made public."

The library is still in the same arrangement as it was according to the instructions of Szepesy. When it moved the collection of Klimó included approximately 33,000 volumes. The individual volumes of the library (with its significant number of books) represent an invaluable treasure, they include extremely rare books, for example, the "Pécsi Missale" from 1499. According to their exclusive binding, the books are housed in the "Golden Room", in the "Parchment Room" or in the "Szepesy Room". The sculpture decoration of the shelves was the handiwork of Mihály Bartalits, a fine master of Pécs. The interior of the library includes the applied art protected Klimó furniture, which can be found in the director's office of the library.

The "Rules" inscribed on marble in 1774, put up on the wall of the corridor, are of particular interest, the last two sentences read as follows: "You don't have to pay anything. Depart enriched, return more frequently."

After resettling the Erzsébet University of Pozsony in Pécs, the old episcopal library was made into the

University library. At present, it is the central library of the Janus Pannonius University of Arts in Pécs. About 400,000 volumes are available to visitors.

Through Bem utca to Kossuth tér

Proceeding along the busy B e m u t c a from Széchenyi square in a southern direction, ecletic houses, built around the turn of the century, line up on the right side. They truly follow the breaks of the former street line (at No. 4 and No. 6). One can discover a certain effort for uniformity and sober moderation on the facades. For example, the hood mouldings above the windows on the floors reflect a certain similarity on each building, only differing somewhat in their details. This also made the line of houses varied and lively, closed by a strange *two storeyed building* in art nouveau style. The carved portal of the shop today: a shoe shop, formerly a pharmacy) in the three storeyed building of *No. 16* is particularly attractive. On the left side, the street leads towards Kossuth tér alongside the *No. 2 University Clinic.*

K o s s u t h t é r to the east of Bem utca is of regular oblong shape. It was artificially developed—on a drawing board. Its present name is due to the statue, which was erected here, earlier (until 1949) it was called Majláth square. The story of the square is short, hardly more than 100 years old. It was built in 1864 from Paulinus utca, the continuation of Kígyó (today: Tímár) utca. Its first name was Új tér (New square), and from the next year Majláth square. Originally, its surroundings were rather underdeveloped, but construction started in a planned manner. The Synagogue—one of the finest art monuments of Pécs built in a romantic style—was in the axis of the oblong shaped regular square. At that time, a long single storeyed line of shops stood on the northern side, called the bazaar of the Good Samaritans. This was pulled down in 1891, and the three storeyed apartment house of the Good Samaritans was built, very successfully in an eclectic style, which today houses various

82

offices. The southern side—as the remnant of the narrow street—was always somehow irregular. The fine shaped building of the "Vadászkürt" (Hunters' Horn) Café and Hotel stood on the corner of Bem utca.

The 100 year old history of the square abounded in events. In 1886, the Pécs Choir held a major festival of choirs, between 1918 and 1921 it was the venue of political events, in 1920 at the mass meeting of the Socialist Party, Gyula Hajdu and Sándor Doktor addressed the masses. A major change occurred in the history of Kossuth tér at the beginning of the 1970s. The southern block was pulled down and the complex of the Konsum Department Store and office building was built.

51 c **Synagogue** (Kossuth tér). Built between 1865—1869, according to the designs of Frigyes Feszl, Károly Gerster and lipót Kauser in a romantic style. The first synagogue of Pécs was built in Citrom utca in 1843, it was used until 1869, and demolished after 1870.

The present building is divided into three. Between the *two* bastion-like *corner projections,* a semicircular finely articulated latticed *middle part* with an excelling gable can be seen, with broad steps to its arched *entrance.* There is a clock in the gable.

The interior decoration and furniture of the synagogue are also valuable, particularly its *organ,* which was the work of the Angster Factory, marked with No. 1.

52 c **Kossuth statue** (Kossuth tér). The bronze statue by János Horvay, stands on a limestone pedestal. It was festively unveiled in 1908, also attended by Ferenc Kossuth. The sculptor, who made most of the numerous Kossuth statues of that period, was born in Pécs.

Janus Pannonius and Geisler Eta utca

The shortest way from Széchenyi tér to István tér leads through J a n u s P a n n o n i u s u t c a. The name of the street was often changed in the past. The

83

name Alejdan (1687) indicates Turkish times, later it was changed to Untere Capitul Gasse (1722), in 1804 it was Akadémia, then Fő Oskola, later Iskola, Oskola street, in 1904 it was named after Kálmán Kardos, the former Lord Lieutenant of Pécs, and finally in 1948 it was named Janus Pannonius utca.

Today, pedestrians are not very keen on it, because it is too busy, and only the northern side is accessible for pedestrians. It is too gloomy, almost like a corrie, with three storeyed buildings on the southern side, buildings that do not fit into a narrow street. However, at the end of the 19th century, the crowns of the trees towering over the stone fence on the site of the present grammar school provided cool shade and the single storeyed baroque house on the site of the present Technical School (Cseh palota) with its simple view and human proportions provided a different atmosphere to the street. It was a refreshening experience to stroll along the street between the main square and the Sétatér (Promenade).

On the way back, the church spire (later demolished) in the axis of the street and the back tract of the church enhanced this atmosphere.

During history, the street always played a significant role in the life of the town. It linked the two centres, the main square of the burgher town and the church centre. It already appeared as an important street on Haüy's known map from 1687. The design about the seige (around 1690), today on display in Vienna, shows a line of houses on the site of the street. Thus it involves one of the oldest streets of Pécs, which was already built up in the Middle Ages. As it was close to the episcopal palace and the cathedral, it was mainly the residence of church officials. The site of No. 2 (today: Inner-city School) was originally, before 1543 the property of the chapter. However, very few traces of the Middle Ages are visible in the street. In the 18th and 19th century, the remnants of the old buildings were all demolished and replaced by new ones. Nevertheless, the gateway of No. 8 still recalls the Middle Ages. There are only 4 such arched gateways in Pécs as the last relics of the pre-Turkish centuries: one of these is the entrance of this house. It is less well known that No. 15 was not so long ago a bath house. The hydropathic establishment of Dr. Vilmos Tolnai operated in the building. The bath house is still extant in the courtyard.

53 c **School** (Janus Pannonius utca 2. or Leonardo da Vinci utca 1). A three storeyed building in eclectic style from 1882. Its predecessor, the two storeyed school may have been built in the Middle Ages. It was still extant in 1686, and it was the residence of Basha Chor Hassan before the expulsion of the Turks. At the beginning of the 18th century, it was a monastery of the Jesuits, then their school. In 1794, the normal (primary) school moved into the building. For a long time, a famous school of decorative arts operated here.

54 c **Former prebendal houses** (Janus Pannonius utca 4, 6 and 8). No. 4 is a two storeyed Baroque apartment building. A two storey house already stood on the site in 1695. Obviously it must have been built in the Middle Ages. In 1720, it was taken over by the chapter and in 1744 Canon Márton Kapuváry built his two storeyed house here, making use of the walls of the medieval building. In 1772, Canon Ferenc Szemenich had it rebuilt and restored. This was when its present appearance was developed. The canon who had the building restored, placed his own and Canon Kapuváry's *coats-of-arms* on the gable above the middle projection. With its decorative *middle projection,* finely carved *gateway* and pleasant *gates,* it is the most representative example of baroque architecture in Pécs.

Janus Pannonius utca 6 is a two storey baroque apartment house. It was built in several phases. In 1720, a low thatched roof building stood on the site. When the tenant left Pécs, there was nobody to tend the building and it became dilapidated, therefore the Chapter froze the income of Canon Miklós Péter Smakers, the owner of the building and used it to completely restore the building in 1765—1767. In the 19th century, (there is no date, but most probably at the beginning of the century), a storey was added to

85

the building. In the 1860s, it became the residence of Canon Jakab Klivényi, a friend of Mihály Vörösmarty, the poet.

The building is asymmetric. The obvious explanation is that later annexes were built. The character of the building is provided by the emphasized double *string cornice,* the *eared windows* with inset frame on the groundfloor and the simple, but noble unframed *windows* on the first floor. The fine and calm, simple facade is a perfect supplement to the animated baroque house at No. 4, and conveys an organic unity to the three prebendal houses.

Janus Pannonius utca 8 is a two storey baroque apartment house. According to data from 1700, a single storey house stood on the site. The present building developed between 1717 and 1747, through various construction work. However, its extensive arched carved stone *gateway* dated back much farther, it is medieval, which confirms that this prebendal house was built with the use of a medieval house, or the medieval gateway—perhaps brought from somewhere else—was built into the house.

The facade is dominated by the extensive gateway. Above it the *ledge* separates the two floors. The groundfloor is horizontally slightly striped and its windows are unframed, while the windows on the first floor are in strip frames. The *gateway* is also attractive as well as the arcaded *courtyard.* Unfortunately, the various annexes spoil the otherwise pleasant effect.

The renowned residents of the house were Canons György Kapucsy and Sándor Fonyó, and Antal Juranics, later Bishop of Győr.

Next to the building, on the site of the present Rose Garden, a granary stood between 1777 and 1894, which was for a long time used as a military uniform store.

55 c   **Building of Csontváry Exhibition.** (Janus Pannonius utca 11—13). The former two storeyed impressive building of the Catholic Young Men's Club, built in 1895 in eclectic style, today houses the paintings of Tivadar Csontváry Kosztka.

The *County Offices of the Federation of Technical and Scientific Societies* and the *Society for the Dissemination of Scientific Knowledge* occupy the ground-floor.

Proceeding from Széchenyi tér to István tér in a south-eastern direction, one has to pass along G e i s l e r   E t a   u t c a. It was known under various names in the past. Sources mention it in 1722, as Obere Schlossgasse, then as Paal street, and Pauli Gasse. Pál street was renamed Apáca utca in 1864. In fact, the nuns of the Order of Notre Dame (Our Lady) lived at the nunnery at the end of the street and built a primary and secondary school next to their nunnery in the 19th century. In 1950, the street was renamed Geisler Eta utca. It is a treasury of historic art monuments.

56 c **The oldest pharmacy in Pécs** (Geisler Eta utca 1). The present house was built in 1897, but according to records, Ágoston Wernischek opened his pharmacy here in 1764. Four years later, he sold the house, the pharmacy and other real estate to György Hölbling. The Hölbling family, after settling in Pécs, remained one of the most renowned families of the town for more than a century.

It was a highly respected family, particularly *Miksa Hölbling,* physician and writer, whose book "Medical description of Baranya County" published in 1845 was a scientifically analyzed description of the county and Pécs. Doctors, historians and ethnographers equally use it as an indispensable source if they deal with this period (19th century). Because of its scientific values, the book appeared in 1980 in facsimile, published by the Health Department of the Baranya County Council.

In 1857, the pharmacy was bought by the Sipőcz family and since then it was called the Sipőcz pharmacy, although the official name, as indicated by its emblem, was "Szerecsen patika" (Saracen Pharmacy).

Its interior is of the end of the last century, when the pharmacy moved into the new house and the old furniture was replaced, already using decorations made in the Zsolnay Factory (for example, the Saracen fountain in the middle of the pharmacy). The furniture is protected and according to plans, the pharmacy will be turned into a museum.

57 c **Geisler Eta utca 3 and 5.** The houses are the most significant examples of romantic architecture in Pécs. Both were built for Miksa Hölbling around 1865. The *gateway* and the *staircase* of No. 5 are extremely grandiose and elegant. Opposite the buildings in romantic style, No. 4 is a long stretched building from around 1777. Its present facade is in neo-classic late baroque style. It continues the building height of the former Czindery and Cséby Houses, and adjoins the former predecessor of the Hungarian National Bank and the Baranya County Library. Its *portal* reflects a Louis XVI style, while its *gateway* relies on pillars.

58 c **Baranya County Library.** The library is housed in two buildings. With regard to its number, the corner belongs to Székesfehérvár utca, however, its main facade faces Geisler Eta utca. This is a two storey building, in late baroque style, built at the end of the 18th century. A *double coat-of-arms* can be seen above the entrance. Today, it is organically linked with Geisler Eta utca 8, which was built after 1798 in late baroque, neo-classic style. It was in the possession of the Baron Bésán, the Országh and Perczel families. After the liberation in 1945, the Baranya County Library took over the building. A *Roman crypt* was found in the courtyard, which was excavated and is on display for visitors.

59 c **Geisler Eta utca 21.** According to recent incorrect opinions, the house was built in an early eclectic style, in the second half of the 19th century—according to archive data it was built in 1775. In fact the house is much older. It was already extant in 1722 in its present dimensions, but probably it was already a reconstructed building.

The *eclectic facade* was obviously added at the end of the century, perhaps exactly after 1885, when it was bought by Miksa Hölbling. Today, a nursery operates in the building.

The bronze statue of *Mihály Babits* was erected in 1980 on the small square in front of the building. The statue of the outstanding poet is the work of Miklós Borsos. The three storey *building of the college* (Geisler Eta utca 23/a) on the small square was the former nunnery of the Order of Our Lady, built in 1847—1851 in neo-classic style. The *nunnery church* was built between 1851—1854 in romantic style, its foundation was festively laid by Prince Primate János Scytovszky.

ISTVÁN TÉR—DÓM TÉR

István tér—or as the people say: Szent István tér or popularly the Promenade—is the second main square of Pécs. In the past it was the centre of the ecclesiastic district. In fact it is not one square. It was united during the planned urbanisation in this century, but even so older people prefer to distinguish the Upper promenade from the Lower promenade, and some call the square in front of the Cathedral: Dóm square. In fact, they were separate entities in the past. The town was surrounded by walls, and walls surrounded the episcopal palace, the Cathedral and the auxiliary episcopal buildings (granary and cellar). Two gateways led into the castle: the Barbican and the one which stood approximately on the site of the present Szepesy statue. A moat surrounded the walls, which were protected by complicated strongholds: earthworks, arcades and stone battlements. A small internal square developed in front of the Cathedral, with the episcopal palace on one side and the ruins of the Szathmáry building on the other. A circular bastion stood on the site of the present Kiosk. The castle gateway was on the southern side with a small building of the guards is front of it.

The town walls of Pécs were known to be very weak. The situation was different with regard to the castle walls. These were well strengthened. During the 1664 campaign, Miklós Zrínyi could not capture it, moreover, the walls resisted the siege in 1696 and the Turks only withdrew from the castle because the water pipeline was blown up.

It was no coincidence that the Lower Promenade developed, it was due to the spread of guns. The defence of the castle would have been difficult with a line of houses in front of the walls. Even if there were some buildings here in the past, they were pulled down when the Turkish threat increased. The Turks, after occupying it, also needed a field of vision, and did not endure buildings which prevented shooting. After the expulsion of the Turks, the western side of the square stretching to the town walls, was completely empty, and the town only parcelled out the plots in 1787. Construction work started, but everything was characterized by the lack of planning. For a time, this was the grain market.

Later, more attention was paid to the square. In 1819, the castle gateway was pulled down, the moat was filled in, and trees were planted. On the eastern part of the lower square. Bishop Klimó erected a fountain in 1750, decorated with a statue of St. George. At the end of the past century, trees were planted and a park was built here. The planning continued in our century, and it reached its peak with the building of the waterfall. In the 20th century, the area was a proper promenade. On Sundays, a military band entertained the promenaders, there was constant effervescence in the Kiosk, and every reputed burgher of the town strolled along the promenade in the forenoon. In the 1920s and 1930s, summer festivals were held in front of the Cathedral, which attracted considerable interest. The ecclesiastic and secular festivities were attended by large crowds. In fact, István tér consists of three squares: the path linking Janus Pannonius and Vak Bottyán streets separate the "Promenade" into Lower and Upper promenades. On the northern part of the Upper promenade, a long line of steps lead up to Dóm square.

Visitors can approach the place from Széchenyi square via Janus Pannonius or Geisler Eta streets, from the museums via Káptalan street and from Sallai street through Vak Bottyán street next to the Barbican. The site is most impressive from the direction of Káptalan street, when the strollers arrive at Dóm square in front of the Cathedral from under the arched passage of Chapter building.

Dóm square is an organic part of István square, lined by the episcopal palace, the Cathedral, the building of the Chapter and the Szepesy statue. When the southern part of the castle walls was still extant, with a gateway within sight of the statue and with the south-eastern circular battlement, there was a completely separate square here. After the gateway, the walls extending on its two sides and the mentioned battlement were pulled down, the square was opened to the south and linked with the "Promenade". This link was made quite clear by the fountain with the St. George statue set up in the axis. However, the basin and the statue were later demolished, then in the thirties the waterfall was completed, planned on the design of Gyula Gosztonyi, which again emphasized the link. The number one task of the waterfall was to attract the eyes from the south directly to the spectacle of Dóm square, to the art monument ensemble of exceptional value, moreover to complete the link with the "Lower promenade". The Cathedral, the Szepesy statue, the broad steps of the "Upper promenade", the waterfall and the romantic nunnery church stood in the axis of the ensemble, and in this way—although to some extent in an artificial manner—created an unparalleled panorama. The intention was to end this artificial character, when in the seventies the painted crypt on the northern end of the waterfall was opened to visitors, and simultaneously the waterfall was demolished. Nevertheless, the object is to maintain the spectacle which emphasizes the unity of the linked squares.

The *Roman and early Christian cemetery* occupied almost the entire area of István square, demarcated by the present Geisler Eta, Székesfehérvár and Janus Pannonius streets. Numerous relics were excavated in the past century. The earliest finds are from the 2nd and 3rd centuries. By that time the Romans ceased to cremate their dead. The graves from the 3rd and 4th centuries are very rich, because objects used by the deceased were buried beside them. Early Christians were buried here from the end of the 3rd century.

The ornamental sepulchre was characteristic of early Christian burial customs.

The first painted crypt was found on the Promenade, more accurately on Dóm square, when pulling down the remnants of the renaissance palace and chapel in 1780. No. 2 crypt was found not far from No. 1 in 1938—1939. By the 1950s, already 10 (No. 1—10), most of them double level, but mainly destroyed crypts were excavated. One of the most significant structures was found in 1922: this is a threefoiled cella trichora, a burial chapel. The sevenfoiled chapel was discovered in 1938—1939 directly beside the eastern side of the Chapter building. Unfortunately, this find of unparelleled value and outstanding from the scientific and artistic viewpoint is not on display, and in fact its exploration was not completed, because it was again covered up.

The square is rich in statues and relics. The statue of *St. Francis of Assisi* by György Bársony can be seen in the mouth of Sallai street, completed in 1939 and erected in 1942. The artist depicted the saint preaching to the birds. The bronze statue stands on a low pedestal, which adjoins a basin. Two pigeons sit on the ledge of the basin, and the saint also holds a pigeon in his hand. People in Pécs call it "Galambos kút" (Pigeon fountain), earlier guides referred to it under this name.

Proceeding to the north from the mouth of the street, the square broadens. In the triangle, created by the forking streets, a *statue "Sisters"* by Pál Pátzai was erected. It was completed in 1942, a limestone statue on a natural stone base, unveiled in 1946.

A *statue* of *Zoltán Kodály* by Imre Varga was unveiled in 1976 on the Lower promenade. The statue on a very small base, on a low counterfort, is turned towards the playground and it seems as if the composer walked among the children, as if he lived and conversed with them.

A broad line of steps lead from the Lower promenade to the Upper promenade. Opposite the steps, in the axis of the southern entrance of the Cathedral, on the site of the demolished gateway of the former Episcopal Castle, the bronze *statue* of *Ignác Szepesy,* a Bishop of Pécs of outstanding merits, was set up, made by György Kiss, the well known sculptor born in Szász-vár. It was unveiled in 1893. It depicts the bishop stepping off the pulpit. Two reliefs are on the two sides of the high base: the one on the right illustrates the foundation of the college, that moment when the designer handed over the designs to the Prelate. In the background, the outlines of the Pollack built Cathedral can be seen. On the left side relief, the artist depicted the event, when the delegation of the town of Pécs handed over the document of gratitude to the founding bishop. The statue, made in an extremely fine manner, is the most outstanding public statue in Pécs.

In the middle of the lawn, alongside the path of the Upper promenade, between the Szepesy statue and the Kiosk, a welded aluminium statue by Sándor Kígyós *"The ballet"* was erected in 1978. The *Csontváry statue* by Jenő Kerényi, faces the entrance of the Csontváry Museum on the other side of the Kiosk. The three-quarter life size bronze statue on a low base, was set up in 1979. The artist depicted the eminent painter in the spirit of his "Self portrait".

From behind the statue, on the eastern side of the promenade, alongside the path leading to the north, there is a *Memorial* in honour of the two world famous musicians: *Prosper Amtmann* and *Imre Weidinger*. This is the second memorial unveiled in 1908. The first one made in 1886 by Mihály Bartalits, a sculptor of Pécs, disappeared without trace.

60 c **Cathedral** (Dóm tér). The best known and most disputed construction of the square—closes the square from an east-west direction. It was presumed from the start of its construction—no written sources or archeological relics were found—that the site of the crypt was an early Christian basilica, then with an annexe towards the west, the present ground plan of the church developed by the 9th century. This was later further expanded and the choir was built over the crypt. The earliest relics originate from the 11th century. The towers were built in the 11th—12th centuries. The entrances to the crypt originate from

93

the 12th century, the folk altar, choir, gallery and carved statues of the colum caps are wnown scientifically as the products of the "Pécs workshop".

The products of Western and local maestros of European significance are today displayed in the romanesque Museum of stonework finds.

The Cathedral burnt down on several occasions. History recorded the fire in 1064. The pacification after the feud of King Solomon and Prince Géza, and the Easter festivities were celebrated at Pécs. On the night of April 11, fire destroyed the Cathedral and the palace. Reconstruction after the fires always involved the transformation and restyling of the church. Obviously, the inflammable plain wooden roof was replaced on such an occasion with Gothic vaulting. Initially the Turks used the church as a stone, then transformed one of the towers into a minaret and used the church as a mosque.

The liberation wars against the Turks left the church relatively intact, but the so-called "devastation by the Rác" caused grave damage to the building, which was then restored by Mátyás Radonay, the first bishop of Pécs after the Turkish time. Bishop Ferenc Nesselrode continued the reconstruction of the church. In fact it was rebuilt in a baroque style, the chapels were drawn under a roof, together with the main nave, and with this a shapeless extensive roof was created.

The interior reconstruction was linked with the name of reputed masters, sculptors and painters, for example, sculptor Sartory, then István Dorfmeister, who painted the Corpus Christi chapel. However, by the end of the 18th century, the cathedral did not comply with requirements concerning its substance and form. The building work carried out at the beginning of the 19th century was headed by Mihály Pollack. Young Pollack —according to the strange request of the client— transformed the exterior of the baroque cathedral into a neo-classic-romantic style church. In its architecture, the interior remained Gothic, the furniture baroque. The reconstruction lasted for a long time, the 12 apostles by sculptor Mihály Bartalits were put on the facade only after several decades, as the completion of the restoration.

It is a disputable question whether the towers would have been left incomplete according to the original idea? A work plan is safeguarded by the Baranya County Archives from the time of the construction work, which shows a pyramid shaped steeple on the top of the towers.

At the end of the 19th century, reconstruction of the church started again, according to the grandiose ideas of Bishop Nándor Dulánszky. The plan was to restore the "original" Cathedral from the Árpád period. The design of the "new" Cathedral was prepared by Friedrich von Schmidt, an Austrian architect, in 1882 and the building work was led by Ágoston Kirstein, completed in 1891. The interior painting was entrusted to eminent artists: Karl Andreä, Moritz von Becherath, Károly Lotz and Bertalan Székely. The sculptures are connected with the names of György Zala and György Kiss. György Zala produced the (less successful) replicas of the wonderful reliefs on the medieval entrance to the crypt, and György Kiss made the recent apostle statues.

The reconstructed Cathedral has a determinative role in the skyline of Pécs. From which ever direction we approach the town, the four spired extensive Cathedral towers over the multitude of houses with its majestic pomp.

It is no coincidence that during the past 100 years it also became the symbol of the town.

On the four corners of the church there are 4 stone helmed twin-windowed *towers*. On two sides they are connected by a line of chapels. The paintings of the *Corpus Christi chapel*, beside the south-western tower, were the handiwork of Károly Lotz. This chapel houses one of the first works of the Hungarian renaissance, the red marble pastoforium of Bishop Szatmáry. The chapel next to the south-eastern tower is named after *Bishop Szent Mór of Pécs*. The murals are the work of Bertalan Székely. They include the famous picture depicting the crowning of King Endre I. The *Mary chapel* on the north-western side was painted by Bertalan Székely, his picture "King Ladislas crosses the Drava" is well known. The *Heart of Jesus chapel* stands on the north-east side with paintings by Károly Lotz.

The Cathedral turns to the square with its side. Its former main entrance and its western facade, which is still finely decorated, overlooks the (still undeveloped) internal square. On the facade of the southern side, the *statues of the apostles* play an outstanding role. The severely damaged statues by György Kiss were replaced by works of modern concept by Károly Antal in 1963. A *composition* by György Kiss can be seen in the spandrel above the main entrance.

The baroque *fountain* by Zsigmond Berényi, surrounded by a fine wrought iron railing (1739) stands alongside the northern wall of the Cathedral.

The present neo-romanesque Cathedral has three aisles with separating pillars and semicircular apses. Its choir is somewhat raised with a large canopied *folk altar.*

Only the main axis of the five-aisled *crypt* under the choir is semicircular. The choir is decorated with paintings of Bertalan Székely, the side apses with those of Károly Lotz.

61 c **Episcopal Palace** (Western side of Dóm tér). The two storeyed neo-renaissance building developed in its present form in the first half of the past century. Commissioned by Bishop János Scytovszky of Pécs (later Archbishop of Esztergom) the design of the reconstruction was made by a talented master of Pécs, Ferenc Windisch. It is the result of his work that the building complex acquired a unified appearance. With this the palace became an important factor in the harmony of the square.

The Palace of the Pécs bishops stood here since King Stephen set up the church. It was built in several stages, but it must have been a significant building already in the 12th century. The medieval building was completely reconstructed in the 15th—16th centuries, in a renaissance style. This is recalled by the fact that the open renaissance staircase was pulled down during the Windisch reconstruction. The Turks moved into the palace and used it for about 150 years. Most probably the palace was severely damaged during the liberation struggles and the siege. First it was only renovated, then the complete reconstruction started, initiated by Bishop György Klimó. The western wing was lengthened to extend it to the 15th century tower. This is where he placed his famous library, which was the first public library in Hungary. The northern and eastern wings were extended with another floor. The entire building was uniformly rebuilt in a Baroque style.

The palace was rebuilt in 1832—1852, in a neo-renaissance style, and its southern phase, with its projection is two storeyed with a *balcony* in the middle, and a gateway with *two* semicircular *doors*. The three storeyed building is closed with a uniaxial corner projection. The southern facade of the building mostly preserved the baroque features, the *double pilaster strips* and the rhythm of the finely framed *windows* breathe the genuine provincial aura of the 18th century. The art monumental value of the Episcopal Palace is indubitable even in its present form after multiple reconstruction.

The large size *Ferenc Liszt statue* by Imre Varga was placed on the counterfort type eastern wall of the southern balcony in 1983.

A complex of annexes belong to the Palace, with the excavated *Gothic chapel* in the rear courtyard, the fortress of the castle and the building (currently under excavation) behind the Cathedral.

The richness of the interior should be mentioned. Primarily the *six* large size *Flemish gobelins* (from Brussels) on the impressive staircase and in the premises of the palace are of interest. They were made at the beginning of the 18th century and Empress Maria Theresa presented them around 1750 to her favourite Bishop György Klimó.

62 c **Chapter archives and parish rectory** (Dóm tér). A two storeyed late baroque building in neoclassic style. It was built in 1784, according to the designs of Sartory, an architect and sculptor of Italian origin. The protruding building on the southern side was designed and built by architect Matthias Fölsinger of Pécs in 1794. The *gable* of the middle projection and the *clock* were completed in the 1880s.

With the construction of the Chapter building, the Dóm square was somewhat enlarged towards the east.

(The Palace built in the 16th century, adjoined the south-eastern tower of the Cathedral, thus standing much more to the west than at present. The renaissance palace, built by György Szathmáry, survived the Turkish occupation, but was seriously damaged during the siege and stood in ruins for almost 100 years. It was pulled down in 1783.) János Krámmer, an architect of Pécs, was commissioned to design the new building, but the construction work was interrupted for some time as the No. 1 painted crypt was discovered at that time, exactly on the planned building site. The next designs were drawn up by Sartory. The three projections on the facade are of different dimensions. The northern corner projection is uniaxial. The groundfloor gateway of the Palace is in fact the entrance to the episcopal sepulchre vault. The wrought iron baroque *gate* was made in 1774. The middle projection is double axial. Broad *steps* lead to both entrances. The *gable* lends a special emphasis to the middle projection. Because of the slope of the square, the southern projection has three levels.

The Palace closes the southern part of Dóm square to the east in a decisive form with its extensive bastion-like mass. The entrance to the Rectory is under the arched passage.

The Pécs Chapter was organized in 1158. It also operated as an authenticating authority (locus credibilis). Its documents from the 18th—19th centuries are preserved by the Baranya County Archives. The Chapter building also houses the highly valuable *clothing collection* of the Pécs bishopric and the *Chapter archives*.

In front of the building (and also on the other side of the square in front of the Episcopal Palace), because of the level drop of the square, a *stone balustrade* was built, the ends of which are closed with monolithic obelisks made of sandstone from Budafa. The coat-of-arms of Bishop Dulánszky were placed on the side of the obelisks. The entrance to the painted crypt is under the eastern balustrade.

The B a r b a k á n k e r t (Barbican garden), namely the promenade leading towards the Barbican is a small park in itself, one of the finest small resting places

98

of an intimate atmosphere in Pécs. With the Barbican in the background, the small round bastion on the castle wall extending along the northern side of the promenade, the pleasant wooden fence on the southern side, and the statue at the end of the road, the whole milieu conveys a renaissance atmosphere. Its benches offer peaceful relaxation and an opportunity for meditation.

63 c   **Janus Pannonius statue** (Barbakán kert). The bronze statue by Miklós Borsos was unveiled in 1972. The broad brim Italian hat covers the face of the life-size figure, thus making it unrecognizable. The carefully finished hand clasps a book. The book—as the symbol of the humanist age—embodies the sciences and literature. In a symbolic manner—hinting at one of the most attractive poems of Janus Pannonius—a small almond tree was planted beside the statue, which lends a particular atmosphere at spring time blooming to the statue, and intimate significance and the fondness of the humanist man for nature.

STREETS IN PLACE OF THE FORMER CIRCULAR LANE

Originally, obviously to make defence safer, a boulevard-like lane surrounded the town within the walls and parallel with them (the present Citrom, Tímár, Liceum, Nagyflórián, Kulich Gyula and Káptalan streets). Later the lane was built up on the right and left, and separated into streets.

One of them, T í m á r   u t c a winds along the south-eastern corner of the town wall. It is no wonder that it was once called Kígyó utca (Snake street). Prior to 1864, before the opening up of Kossuth tér, it stretched from present Bem utca to Kossuth Lajos utca.

At some time in the past, this was the most infamous part of Pécs. The residents of present Kossuth tér and Líceum street frequently complained that their street "... is full of libertines and taverns... that all honest and moral individuals leave in abhorrence".

99

Later, even the name of the street was changed. Its new and final name was connected with the former Höffler tannery, which operated in this street (on the corner of present Bercsényi street—today the PIK office building) until the end of the last century.

The northern continuation of Tímár utca is L í - c e u m   u t c a that leads into Kossuth Lajos utca alongside the present Széchenyi Grammar School, the former Liceum (hence its name).

64 c **Former outhouse of the Paulites** (Liceum utca 4). Later the building of the Liceum printing house. At present, used as the office building of ME-GYESZER. It was built in 1762 in a baroque style, with a pavilion-like solution. It is a building on two levels, a corner building with mansard, with ground-floor wings adjoining its two sides.

65 c **Liceum utca 7.** An apartment house, built in 1823 on two floors in neo-classic style. In the eighties, the owner resident was Endre Taray, an MP. The facade of the building is divided by a slightly protruding *string-course* with *cantilevered main cornice* above the floor. The three middle windows on the first floor are placed in an inset panel with an articulated *parapet* above the crowning and above this, semicircular gables over the windows. The hood moulding of the two far windows on the first floor are cantilevered. The gateway is segment-arched.

Liceum street, which leads into Kossuth Lajos street, continues to the north in N a g y f l ó r i á n   u t c a. In the past, it was the residence of well-to-do craftsmen. Where the street meets Déryné street, it widens into a small square. This is F l ó r i á n   t é r, with the *Szent Flórián statue* by Erzsébet Kozma, erected in 1926. Saint Flórián was the patron saint not only of the firemen, but also of the town of Pécs, this is the explanation why so many Flórián statues are to be seen in the town. The present one was not the first on this site. The first was erected in the middle of the square in 1825.

Nagyflórián street leads to K u l i c h   G y u l a
u t c a at the north-eastern corner of the town wall.
No. 22 was the "Matessa orphanage", a foundation by
István Matessa. This building houses the Transdanubian Scientific Institute of the Hungarian Academy
of Sciences. The street abounds in historic art monuments. The date 1781 above the carved stone framed
gateway of the *corner house* at the mouth of Zetkin
Klára utca indicates this: very old houses line the
street. One of them is the two storeyed *neo-classic
building* of the management of the former episcopal
estate from 1816. Before 1950, the street was called
Papnövelde utca (Seminary street).

66 c **Former Seminary.** The extensive complex of
the seminary was built in several phases. The
Kluich Gyula street wing was built between 1742—
1746, based on the designs of András Petz, an architect of Pécs. The foundation stones were festively
laid by Zsigmond Berényi. In 1791, the building was
extended towards the east, as designed by Mátyás
Fölsinger. Bricklayer, Farkas Retzenwinkler, was
entrusted with the construction work. In 1883, the
western wing—and the chapel—were completed. This
is when the door frame from the Heart of Jesus
Chapel of the old Cathedral, the work of Péter Gian-
none, a stone mason of Pécs, from 1793, was built into
the new construction.

The north-western wing is in eclectic, the old one
in baroque style. The southern facade is articulated
by a *pilaster strip* at its full height. The levels are
separated by *string courses,* the windows are framed
with *hood moulding* above them. The centre of the
facade is the richly carved *gateway* with the coats-of-
arms of Bishop Berényi and the Pécs Chapter, and
decorated with the statue of St. Paul. The building
indicates a kinship with the former Jesuit monastery
(Asztalos College) on Széchenyi square.

The two storeyed 18th century baroque building of
the *Small seminary* faces the complex. On its courtyard, the former tenant Abbot Dániel Hersching transformed the outhouse into an "ornamental building"
in 1797. He put up his carved coat-of-arms on the

southern facade of the small neo-classic baroque building.

The former Seminary and the undecorated former County Hall are linked with a two storeyed 18th century *apartment building,* which at the same time closes the small square, created by the approach to the County Hall.

67 c   **Old County Hall** (later District County Hall, today: Directorate of the Baranya County Museums, Kulich Gyula utca 5). It was built in three phases. The plot was bought by the county in 1731. The three storeyed main block on six axes of the County Hall was built the same year. The string cornice between the floors is particularly powerful between the first and second floor. The panels between the windows are articulated by *pilaster strips* on the two floors, on the edge in doubles. Above the first floor windows, the *gable* is of uneven line. The *gateway* with herma pillars and the coat-of-arms—is particularly attractive. According to the inscription, it was installed in 1772.

Later the County Hall proved to be too small. The county wanted to sell it, and instead bought the former Paulite monastery in Kossuth (then Fő) street, but the reconstruction—because of the intervention of the bishop—did not take place. Then the extension of the County Hall was decided on. This took place in 1885. The eclectic wing on 13 axes successfully and harmoniously fits in a broken line to the baroque main building. The wing adjoining the northern side of the baroque main building, which houses the *assembly hall,* was completed in 1930. The fine *wrought iron work* of the new building and courtyard entrance was the handiwork of János Bizse, an ironsmith of Pécs.

Kulich Gyula street leads to Hunyadi road, and opposite on the other side of the road, K á p t a l a n u t c a begins. At the mouth of the street, where a small fountain stood in the Middle Ages (which is confirmed), the bronze *statue of St. John the Baptist* by Elek Lux was set up in 1942. above an open framed plain basin. Káptalan street is one of the oldest in Pécs. All its buildings are historic art monuments. Not even the name of the street has changed in the past 300 years. According to archeological excavations, many more houses lined the street in the Middle Ages, making it zig-zag. Two medieval buildings are extant: No. 2 and No. 4.

68 c **Káptalan utca 2.** The first records about the building originate from 1324. Provost István Korkácsi Pálfia owned the house. The present middle —entrance—part was the provost's house in the Middle Ages. In 1476, Provost Zsigmond Hampó set up Hungary's first public library in this house. In 1520, István Brodarics rebuilt the building in a renaissance style and had the facade painted. During the Turkish occupation, a Mohammedan Turkish high priest lived in the building. Two designs were preserved from the time after the expulsion of the Turks, the building appears on both, with a tower over its arched gothic entrance. Its present structure allows us to presume that there was a tower.

In 1702, the Chapter started legal proceedings to recover the building. It won the case in 1726. Provost Miklós Givovich extended the house towards the west and placed his coat-of-arms, decorated with a Mary statue, above the gateway. In 1820, further restorations took place. The baroque loggias on the first floor were rebuilt into rooms. The next major reconstruction was carried out in 1844 by Antal Piatsek. Later, already in the 20th century, minor and major renovations took place. In 1937, Gyula Gosztonyi revealed the baroque details.

During the exploration and restoration of 1954—1955, the medieval parts were made visible. In addition to the already known *two Gothic arched gateways* and the *niche* in the *gateway,* a *window* with a *resting bench* on the first floor, *a spy hole, remnants of the facade painting, and fragments of the renaissance window frame* were discovered.

At present, the *Zsolnay memorial exhibition of the Janus Pannonius Museum* occupies the upper floor of the building.

The *corner building* is in neo-classic style, opposite the former Provost house, and was built according to the designs of Josef Piatsek in 1838. It was one of the smallest prebendal houses, it was later extended.

After the last artistic restoration, the *permanent exhibition of Victor Vasarely,* an artist of international fame, was opened in the building.

69 c **Former prebendal house** (Káptalan utca 4.). During the restoration which ended in 1978, a large number of 15th century, medieval relics were found (Gothic tracery windows, with a seat on the inner side). After the Turks, Canon Gábor Bakich rebuilt the house at his own expense, almost transforming it from its foundations. A *marble plaque* dated 1730 commemorates the building work.

On the eastern side of the building, above the carriage drive, a middle projection with a mansard can be seen, on the corner Bakich built a small pavilion, with the house shapel on the first floor.

At present the building is a *museum,* where the paintings of *Béla Uitz* are on display. The modern gallery is on the first floor of the building.

70 c **Káptalan utca 5.** The first data about the building originate from 1749—1766 when the middle part of the house was erected. However, this does not exclude the possibility that it was built over medieval walls or foundations. The prebendal house was extended in 1790 towards the east, that was the time when the gateway and staircase were built.

It is a building with a simple and calm facade, and it is a fine complex. The attractive *end facade* of the building plays a dominant role in the street.

The gateway and the staircase have a pleasing appearance, they were little effected by recent renovations, which in fact spoilt the facade. At present, the exhibition of the painter, Endre Nemes, can be visited in the building.

71 c **Prebendal house (Káptalan utca 6.).** The plot on which No. 6 and No. 8 are situated was divided in 1833. The stables and the garden of the castle's parson stood on the plot of present No. 8. The No. 6 house reflecting neo-classic elements was built in 1841 by Ferenc Windisch, a well known architect of Pécs. However, at the end of the century, it was completely rebuilt in an eclectic style, according to the design of Ágoston Kirstein. Access to the buiding is under a double pillared *portico* in front of the three axial middle projection, protruding from the facade. The entrance still demonstrates the traces of the former neo-classic building. In arched niches on the two sides, *statues* by György Kiss can be seen. A *balcony* with balustrade was built over the portico. The facade is articulated by broad stone *pilaster strips* and the windows are *frome arched*.

An *exhibition* of the graphic works by painter *Ferenc Martyn*, occupies the groundfloor of the building.

THE NORTH-EASTERN PART OF THE INNER-CITY

The most densely populated part within the town walls was situated to the north from present Széchenyi square and Kossuth Lajos street. Today, it includes the following streets: Kulich Gyula, Nagy Flórián, Kis Flórián, Megye, Anna, József, János, Déryné and Zetkin Klára (some of them were already described as part of the circular lane). Many old buildings were pulled down in this area, but undoubtedly the largest number of low adobe houses from the 18th and 19th centuries survived here.

Déryné utca changed most. No. 27—a baroque corner house—is perhaps the only one from the 18th century. It is known that Mrs. Déry appeared on the stage on several occasions in Pécs, but never in the former, since then demolished stone theatre of Mária utca (today Déryné utca). Nevertheless, the renaming of the street in 1956, where the theatre stood at that time, showed the respect towards the great Hungarian actress.

No. 9 and No. 11, the building of the former DGT (Danube Steam Shipping Company) is today occupied by the *Mecsek Mining Museum*. The theatre of the

Pécs Ballet is in the former building (No. 18) of the Charitable Women's Association.

72 c **Majláth House** (Déryné utca 11—13). The historic art monument building is the most characteristic representative of early classic style in Pécs. The complex of the two buildings dominates the street. Most probably they were built after 1786, for this was the time when the Petrovszky family bought the plot. In 1845, it was bought by judge György Majláth, and since then it has been named after him.

The ionic crowns of the *pilaster strips* and the *garland ornaments* indicate late baroque, while the horizontal and vertical *elements* of the *facade* indicate a change to neo-classic.

The line of buildings, which starts with the parish building in M e g y e k ö z and continues with No. 7, 9, 11 and 13 M e g y e u t c a, play a particular role in the skyline of the inner-city. The seemingly chaotic line of the buildings lends a magic appearance to the strange way—unplanned manner—of Pécs architecture. No. *11* and *13* represent the characteristic type of urban architecture. They are an example of how the houses built at an angle to the street developed parallel with the street. When the fences were pulled down, the appearance of the street lost most of its harmony. The *parsonage* (Megye köz 1) was built in neo-classic eclectic style, *Megye utca 7/1.* in romantic style and behind it on the same plot *Megye utca 7/2* is a baroque building. Most probably part of the house already existed in 1702, later it was reconstructed (perhaps after 1737) and extended. Abbot Zsigmond Hersching from Madocsa placed his dated coat-of-arms above the entrance in 1782. *Megye utca 9* already existed in 1722, (that part of the house at an angle with the street). The present, late baroque facade was built in the 18th century. The part of *Megye utca 11*, to the right of the gateway, at an angle to the street, already stood in 1722. The building developed into its present form in a gradual manner, its facade was built in neo-classic late baroque. *Megye utca 13*, a single storeyed eclectic building was most probably built earlier. The ensemble is closed by the *Megye-lépcső* (County steps) built in 1837.

73 c **Megye utca 18.** A particularly valuable baroque building. In 1737, it was the residence of Mihály Horváth, the magistrate of the town. It is a very early baroque house, although it was rebuilt on several occasions. Recently, it was spoilt when the relocation of the *gateway* made the building asymmetric.

THE FORMER WALLS

The town of Pécs and the internal castle were most probably surrounded by walls in the 13th century. The construction work must have tallied with the process initiated by the king after the Tartar invasion (1241—1242), with the aim of preventing further unexpected devastation and to ensure the protection of the inhabitants. Similarly to the other Hungarian towns, Pécs built its wall system at that time.

The walls already had two vulnerable points: they surrounded a too large area, thus requiring a vast defensive force, and from the high hills on the east, the enemy could easily overlook and shoot at the castle. After the appearance of firearms, the low and narrow town and castle walls, which had no foundations, completely lost their strategic significance, that in fact was not necessary in the 13th to 15th centuries, because the town situated in the interior of the country, was not threatened by any danger. After the weakening of the central power (after the death of King Matthias in 1490) the defensive power of the country was highly weakened. Because of the danger of Turkish attacks, the town walls needed strengthening. There was no money, nevertheless, some building work was done on the castle walls. Allegedly the gate bastion, the barbican was built under the supervision of Pál Kinizsi and external battlements were also built around the castle.

After the defeat at Mohács (1526), the Turkish threat increased and public law and order deteriorated. After the election of dual kings, the state of anarchy dominated in the country. There were no forces or money available. After the loss of the southern defensive line, the situation of Pécs became critical. King Ferdinand I gave the town temporary exemption from taxation in 1528 in return for the promise that the citizens of the town will fortify the walls and defence works. This must have brought little result, because in 1543 the Turks occupied the town and the castle of Pécs almost without a sword blow.

During the Turkish domination, the condition of the walls continued to deteriorate. After the loss of Szigetvár (1566), nobody bothered about the conditions of the walls any more. However, in the 17th century the Turks did some repair to the castle wall. Most probably, they pulled down the houses in front of the castle wall and freed the area of present István square. Strengthening the castle walls in this way it could resist the attack of Miklós Zrínyi in 1664. But the town walls had no significance. It was easy for the troops of Zrínyi to occupy them and later János Makár attacked the town on several occasions. It was easily occupied by the allied army in 1686. In 1704, the „Kuruc" and later the „Rác" troops penetrated the town without resistance.

All significance of the walls ceased after 1711. In order to promote traffic, they were broken on various (9) points, the 4 town gateways were pulled down, together with the gateway of the Bishop Castle, then the area was divided into plots, the moats were filled in together with the areas inside the walls. Unfortunately, a considerable part of the walls was pulled down in the second half of the 19th century, nevertheless, based on designs, etchings and the still extant remnants, the town walls can almost perfectly be reconstructed. In 1687, Josef Haüy surveyed the walls with an architect's precision, together with the network of the connecting streets.

The excavation of the castle walls and restoration started in the 1970s. At present, the castle walls are completely freed and most of them are excavated and restored art monuments.

The town wall is also excavated and restoration is being carried out.

The town and castle walls of Pécs are almost unparalleled intact medieval constructions in Hungary. They are perhaps the most interesting spectacle in the town, which is rich in historic art monuments. The Barbican and the western and northern fortress system of the castle, and the wall system behind the barbican garden link the episcopal palace, the Cathedral and the prebendal building into a unique ensemble of historic art monuments, visible not only from the direction of István square — from the south — but also from the west and north. It is particularly fascinating from Landler Jenő street: the restored Barbican and the surrounding fortress system, the medieval tower and the baroque western wing of the episcopal palace.

The monotony of the northern and western walls is pleasantly broken by five round and square bastions, built closely alongside each other. The large mass of the Cathedral appears from behind the wall, with its sparkling whiteness. The northern unrestored side of the town wall has a pleasant atmosphere, with the highly towering round bastion in Vak Bottyán street, and the picturesque small bastion at the end of Kulich Gyula street. The bastion and the stretch of the wall in Citrom street was recently excavated and after its restoration it will be one of the finest spectacles in the neighbourhood of Jókai street. Further fragments of the walls can be seen in Landler Jenő street, at the beginning of Rákóczi road, and in Eötvös street. The wall in Felsőmalom street is still covered by houses.

IN THE SUBURBS

The suburbs most probably already developed in the Middle Ages around the town — surrounded by walls. They already had a church in the 13th century, for the All Saints Church was built at that time. The Tettye brook with abundant water flowed behind the Gothic church, and it supplied a number of mills with water energy. During the Turkish occupation, most of the Hungarian inhabitants of the town settled around the church. This was when the Budai suburb developed. After the spread of the Reformation, this was the only church of the Christians in Pécs. However, the initial unity was soon dissipated. It was the venue of religious polemics, the so-called "Pécs dispute" in 1588, between the Unitarian György Válaszúti and Máté Skaricza of the Reformed Church.

According to etchings from Turkish times, the Budai suburb was surrounded by palings. György Szathmáry, the Bishop of Pécs, built his renaissance summer resort at the beginning of the 16th century to the north of this district — obviously in the episcopal game park — and later the Turks turned it into a dervish monastery. Since then, the area was called Tettye. After the expulsion of the Turks, the Hungarians moved into the town, and were replaced by the baptised Mohammedan Bosnians, who earlier settled in Pécs. They set up the closed settlements of "Barátúr környéke", "Zidina környéke" and the "Benga" — as explained earlier. The houses were built in an unplanned manner, and strangers could easily lose their way in the winding alleyways and closes, among the irregularly built houses.

Parallel with the increase in the size of the town, the Budai suburb extended towards the south. The simple houses of Felsővámház utca (Custom's House street) and Pálya utca (today: Zsolnay Vilmos) were built and as the result of the 19th century industrialisation, the area became more densely populated and poorer. With time, the Budai suburb started to extend to the north. Hungarians and Bosnians mainly engaged in viticulture, they built their houses leaning on the castle wall, alongside Kálvária (today: Vak Bottyán) and Petrezselyem streets (today: Aradi vértanúk útja). Building work also started to the north (Jozafát valley) beyond the Kaposvári Gate.

In the 18th century, a densely populated settlement developed to the west of the Szigeti Gate. In fact the development already started during the Turks. The mosque of Pasha Hassan Jakovali was built alongside the walls in the mid-16th century with the monastery of the Merlev dervish order. There was a cemetery beside the mosque. The Turkish cemetery was somewhat further away, at the foot of the Rókus Hill, with the sepulchre (turbe) of the hermit Turkish soothsayer, Baba Idris.

The Szigeti suburb became inhabited in the first half of the 18th century. Mostly Hungarians engaged in agriculture settled here. The rich Megyer-puszta was situated to the south of the suburb, rented by Pécs burghers and noblemen from the Treasury for long decades. It was a source of the town's riches. To the north, abundantly yielding vineyards were situated: Makár Hill, Donátus, Arany Hill, Bálics and Frühweis.

Significant manors developed in the suburb. The best known belonged to Canon and Grand Provost Sándor Fonyó, who bequeathed his outhouses to the town. Finally, the building was used by the army. Its name indicates this: Stock-ház (prison).

Outside the walls, the town built a tavern and a road house. Later, this became the famous "Százéves" (Hundred year old). The "Csillag" (Star) road house, to the west of it, was also well known.

The Xavér Church was built in the 18th century, one of the finest relics of baroque architecture in Pécs.

Until the end of the 19th century, the western border of Pécs was the Stock-house. However, as a result of industrialisation, the town started to increase in this direction. Prior to the First World War, three barracks were built: Franz Joseph I (behind the Stock-

111

house), the Hussar and the artillery barracks. The Cadet school was built in 1897—1898, based on the design of Ignácz Alpár (today: the buildings of the Medical University stand on the site). The drill ground was situated in front of the barracks—in fact at the foot of Makár Hill—stretching to Rácváros, which from 1930 onward was used as the airport of Pécs. The hangar, which the retreating Germans blew up in 1944, stood at the end of present Endresz György utca. The street was named after the Hungarian pilot, who together with navigator Sándor Magyar, flew in 1931 from Harbor Grace in North America to Hungary, creating with this two world records: he make the best average speed and the longest route over the continent following the ocean. The hangar and airport were connected with Szigeti road via Pilóta street. The horse race course with the tribune was situated to the south of the airport, directly along the railway line. In addition to horse races, it was the venue of the tournaments of the paramilitary youth organisation, gymnastic competitions and parades. The Kovács settlement was built in the first half of the 20th century, to the west of the airport, consisting of small single level houses.

There were hardly any factories or workshops in the Szigeti suburb. Only the Brewery set up in 1854 could be mentioned.

The youngest of Pécs' three suburbs is the Siklósi. Initially, the well-to-do Pécs burghers built their outhouses and manors to the south of the Siklósi Gate. This is indicated by the name of the street: „Pajta" (Barn)—later Majláth street. Endre Madarász, the father of the famous Hungarian painter, built his iron plant (today: the Leather Factory) at the Stone Bridge, alongside the highway leading to Siklós.

The railway station of Pécs was built at the end of the 19th century. A broad avenue was built from Ország út (today: Rákóczi út) to the railway station (Indóház utca—today: Szabadság út). This is a consciously planned road, with the four spired Cathedral and the green slope of the Mecsek in its axis. In 1907, the Zsolnay statue was erected at the end of the road, on its

The turbe of Baba Idris in Nyár utca

The SZOT Holiday Resort

A baroque gateway in Rácváros

The French memorial in the Mecsek

Vineyards

Bird's eye view of Újmecsekalja (Uránváros)

Lvov suburb with the Educational Centre in the background

The theatre hall of the Educational Centre

The artificial ice rink

The guesthouse of the Baroque castle at Úszög

The ruins of the former Paulite monastery on the Jakab mountain

The medieval church at Pécs-Málom

The new rest centre of Pécs under the Málom

eastern side the villas of the Schlauch colony and the Reformed Church.

Pécs underwent a dynamic development in the mid-1950s. This is when the Meszesi housing estate, the lower phase of Jókai street, and on the site of the former airport the Uranium Town (officially: Újmecsekalja) were built. During the 1960s, construction started in the southern township, under the old Kertváros. By the beginning of the 1980s, it developed into a district with 30,000 inhabitants.

During its development, the town also absorbed the former small villages: Mecsekszabolcs, Vasas and Somogy, Rácváros and Ürög, Cserkút, Kővágószőlős, Hird and Málom are all part of Pécs today.

THE BUDAI SUBURB

74 A   **All Saint Church** (at the meeting of the Tettye and Sörház utca). The oldest building of the Budai suburb is situated on a small hill on the road leading to Tettye. It is surrounded by a castle-wall like fence, the fence of the former churchyard. The church was built in the 13th century, it was single aisled. In the 15th century it was reconstructed in a late Gothic style. This is when the square ended choir was demolished. The new choir was supplied with buttresses. During the Turkish occupation, this was the only church for the Christians to use and this was the venue of the famous religious dispute of 1588. In the 18th century the church was again reconstructed into a three aisled church, and this was when the small *tower* with its bulbiform cupola was built.

The road towards Tettye leads along the steps of the church. A *memorial plaque* can be seen on the wall of the extensively reconstructed house of T e t t y e u t c a 47. In fact this was the editorial offices of the extremely significant newspaper "Munkás" (Worker) since 1898.

The surroundings of T e t t y e t é r are the most popular rest park and entertainment complex of Pécs.

In the past, the famous paper mill founded by Bishop György Klimó stood at the beginning of the square. The lower and upper squares are separated by a road.

Since the turn of the century, the Tettye has been the favourite excursion spot of Pécs citizens. The first *running course* and *football pitch* of Pécs were built in front of the ruins. Organised by "Gyuri Reéh" the legendary alderman of the town, major festivities were held here. Memorable May Day celebrations took place under the cool foliage of the trees. The famous arboretum, the *Pintér-kert*, with its rare plants, can be seen on the western side of the square.

75 A   **The Garden of Ruins** (the upper part of Tettye tér). György Szathmáry built his renatissance summer resort between 1505—1521 somewhat further from the town—most probably in the middle of his game park. The building had two storeys. Today, its former brilliance can only be guessed from the ruins, and from one or two excavated carved stones. The Turks used it as a dervish monastery. After their expulsion, the building was in a relatively good condition. At the beginning of the past century, its stones were taken away and used for the urban construction work. Since the turn of the century, the crumbling walls were placed under protection.

From Tettye a slightly rising road leads to H a v i - h e g y with an unparalleled beautiful view of the town. Along the road, on the top of a cliff, the *crucifix* by Sándor Rétfalvi can be seen.

76 A   **Chapel of Havi-hegy.** According to historic data, the citizens of Pécs made a pledge during the great Black plague of 1690 that if the danger passed, they will erect a memorial chapel on top of Havi-hegy. During the next year, they fulfilled their promise. They carried the building material by hand to the top of the hill. Later the small chapel was extended, and after the fire of 1780, it was rebuilt in Louis XVI style.

The extremely simple church has a significance from the viewpoint of the skyline of the town, it is an indispensable part of the Pécs panorama. The view of the town and the distant suburb are enchanting from Havi-hegy, but the most fascinating are the small houses and winding streets at the foot of the mountain, in the valley of the Tettye brook and on the slopes. It is a picturesque spectacle. From a distance, the houses look like beautiful, small toys. The playful chaos of the roofs, trees, drying laundry, the splashing brook on the road, the extensive roof of the former mill, its porch and wrought iron fence, carved ledges, natural stone walls and strangely crooked chimneys, provide an unparalleled sight.

Returning to the town along Tettye utca, we reach Vak Bottyán utca at the old *Czenger barracks*. The road along the freed town wall stretches to Á g o s -t o n   t é r. The Augustinian friars settled down at Pécs in 1710. They built their monastery on the eastern side of the square, today this is the *Rectory*. They built their *church,* with the use of the remnants of the Turkish mosque, which stood in front of the monastery. The in fact baroque church was reconstructed in 1912 in an eclectic style. The former monastery is a baroque building.

The lower stretch of S ö r h á z   u t c a starts to the south of the square. The *corner building* on the even side is a characteristic example of the tanneries with drying lofts. The opposite corner house was built as a higher elementary school in early eclectic style. Earlier the brewery stood in the street, which explains its name. The existence of the brewery was due to the abundant water of the Tettye brook. The brook was of major significance in the life of Pécs. When the town was surrounded by walls, a rapid mill brook with plenty of water flowed along the eastern moat, from the Tettye to the south. Mills lined its banks. Under the Tettye, between the mills, almost thrown onto to each other, small sheds stood on the bank. These were the tool sheds of the tanners. They used the water to soak the skins. The line of mills continued to the south of the Budai Gate. At the beginning of the 19th century, considerable tanneries developed here (Krautszak, Erreth and Höffler).

115

The houses between the castle wall and the brook formed a street by this time: this became F e l s ő - m a l o m   u t c a (Upper mill street). Among the major tanneries, the cobblers and furriers guilds also had their houses here, in fact the entire valley of the mill brook was the first "industrial area" of Pécs. It was not an elite street, but the landlords—naturally the richest burghers of the town—built houses worthy of their wealth. Therefore, a very strange picture developed in Felsőmalom street. The exterior of the houses was high ranking and elegant, but towards the backyard, where the mill stream flowed and the workshops were situated—where the skins were soaked and tanned and dried—dirt and stench covered everything.

In the first half of the past century, several new buildings were erected in the street. No. 7 built by József Piatsek, the famous architect of the town, is a historic art monument today. The southern part of the street was lined by single storeyed baroque houses, which disappeared in the recent past. No. *16/1* is an insignificant building from the outside, but its columned entrance hall is very grandiose, "of municipal standards". It is regrettable that its romantic facade was twice reconstructed at the beginning of the century.

Felsőmalom street is very rich in *historic art monument houses*. No. 3, 7 and 10 were built in neo-classic and No. 9 in baroque, but its later built annexes are again in neo-classic style. No. 11 is in neo-classic late baroque, No. 19 in baroque, and No. 21 in eclectic style.

One of the highest ranking buildings of modern architecture is situated on the corner of Felsőmalom street and Rákóczi road. The originally three storeyed *apartment building* was designed by Alfréd Forbáth. Later an additional floor was built onto the building. Fortunately, this addition did not spoil the proportions and qualities of the apartment house.

77 c   **Tanner House** (Felsőmalom utca 9.). Built in 1774. At that time, the largest tannery occupied the building. Later, a restaurant and a dance house were opened in the back part of the building, naturally for the entertainment of the poorer urban dwellers. According to traditions, it had a good cuisine (although the penetrating stench of the tannery could not be a very palatable incentive for the hungry guests). On April 2, 1985 the new museum of Pécs was opened in this building with the exhibition "The history of Pécs between 1686—1948".

ON RÁKÓCZI ÚT TO THE SZIGETI SUBURB

Felsőmalom utca ends at one of the most important junctions of R á k ó c z i ú t. Road No. 6, which also includes Rákóczi út, turns to the south here, and passes through the town along Rózsa Ferenc, then Szalai András streets, and through the new town centre. Rákóczi út (former Ország út) encircles the formerly walled inner-city. It was always of major importance, all transit traffic through Pécs was carried by it. During the development of capitalism, its role increased. Arching around the inner-city, the road turns to the west at Kórház tér (Hospital square), and leads through the Szigeti suburb, then through the former Rácváros towards Szentlőrinc, Szigetvár.

K ó r h á z t é r is an important junction of the town, similarly to the past. This is where the transit traffic bypasses the inner-city and meets the traffic coming down from the vineyard hills. An old town gate, the Szigeti Gate, stood on the eastern, deeply inset side of the square. A *part* of the *town wall* can be seen here. The new *Pannónia Hotel* is built behind the wall.

78 c **Mosque of Pasha Hassan Jakovali** (Rákóczi út 2) was built outside the Szigeti Gate in the mid-16th century. At present, it is pressed between the buildings of the hospital, but in the past it stood alone. It stands in a conventional direction turned towards the south-east and its groundplan is a regular square. The facade is closed by a ledge, which holds an octagonal drum wall, with a window on each side.

117

A dome-shaped *cupola* sits on the drum. The simple unadorned facade is articulated by two triple arched windows. The entrance hall covered by a line of cupolas joined the north-western side and was most probably pulled down at the time when the hospital was built.

The *minaret* adjoins the right corner of the building, it is the original up to the circular balcony, above the balcony it is a replacement.

After the Turks were driven out, Bishop Nesselrode of Pécs turned the mosque into a chapel between 1702—1732 (Nepomuki Szent János chapel). The exterior of the building was reconstructed in a baroque style and an interior gallery for the choir was built. This is when the entrance hall was pulled down and the then single storeyed hospital was joined to the chapel. The restoration of first the mosque, then chapel started in 1956. It was somexhat freed from the pressure of the adjoining buildings, the baroque annexes were demolished and the original floor level was restored.

In 1971—1972 the remnants of the former dervish monastery, adjoining the complex of the mosque, were excavated, and the original entrance restored. The prayer alcove (mihrab) was restored.

During the restoration, the mosque was built for its original purpose. A *permanent exhibition* of Turkish (Mohammedan) relics, found in Hungary, is displayed in the foyer on the site of the original entrance hall and dervish monastery.

The mosque is surrounded on two sides by the buildings of the *County Hospital.* The southern two storey building, the former Rudolfineum was built in the mid-19th century in a very simplified romantic style. The *building* on the northern side is directly linked with the mosque. It was built by Bishop Nesselrode in 1714 over the entrance hall of the Turkish mosque and over the foundations of the monastery walls. In 1714, it was built as a single storey building, in 1780 it was extended, and the floor was built over it. In 1868—1869 another floor was added and in 1924 it was turned into a four level building. In 1894—1895 it was extended towards Garay utca.

79 c   **Former "Magyar Korona" Hotel** (Doktor Sándor utca 2). The two storey baroque building closes the square from the north. The hotel was built by the town after 1768. There was no tavern owned by the town in the Szigeti suburb, therefore, a plot was bought in 1768, directly at the gate, and the building of the cellar, then the tavern started immediately. As the building became a road house, there were stables and coach houses built in the courtyard, and a small blacksmith's foundry on the corner. At present, the former baroque hotel and the small workshop, with their fine proportions, are an important part of the square.

It is difficult to examine the somewhat noisy and too busy square in detail, but the romantic corner houses, which open Sallai and Doktor Sándor streets —are noteworthy. They are significant examples of romantic and eclectic architecture in Pécs.

Doktor Sándor utca considerably widens towards the high building, because of the modern demolitions. A significant centre of the currently built housing district developed here. Two outstanding buildings of the slowly evolving square are the former two storeyed arcaded baroque *Griffaton building,* today the Várkonyi Nándor juvenile library of the Pécs urban library, and the Stock-house. They are fine examples of how old buildings can organically fit into a completely modern and new housing estate, providing a refreshening atmosphere to the monotonous new.

80 c   **Stock-ház** (Nagy Jenő utca 38). It had a lively past. The site of the former Turkish cemetery was bought by Canon György Kapucsy in 1714. Later, he left it to his nephew, Canon Sándor Fonyó, titular bishop and Grand Provost of Pécs. Unexpectedly, Fonyó left the plot, not to the chapter, but to the town, on the condition that an alms house should be set up in the house he built on the ground in 1762. After his death, the town inherited the building in 1767. Most probably, the date 1767 was added to the apex of

119

the entrance in homage to Fonyó. First the town wanted to open a tavern in the building, but the violation of the conditions of the will caused complications. It came handy to the town that it had to provide accommodation for the future military command. This building was destined for the purpose. The commander, His Highness General Koburgh, lived here in 1767. When the command was withdrawn, the building was turned into a military prison. From that time on it was called Stock house—which means prison.

It is a single storeyed baroque corner house with mansard and a solid tower adjoining the building on its north-western corner. It was rebuilt on several occasions. During one restoration—in our century—the roof windows above the mansard windows were covered up.

A significant art monument of the Szigeti suburb is the small baroque *chapel,* named after *Saint Francis Xavier,* which in A l k o t m á n y u t c a can be seen today in a new and modern milieu. The modern houses frame the small square, which with the church, add to the intimate atmosphere. Here and in the neighbourhood of Petőfi square, the buildings perfectly supplement each other. The Xavier Church was built directly after the Turks left the country and its present form was added in 1739.

81 A **The turbe of Baba Idris** (Nyár utca). The lone standing art monument of the suburb can be seen in the courtyard of the Children's Hospital. It is due to a coincidence that the sepulchre (turbe) of Baba Idris, the Holy man of the Turks, survived the storms of history. In fact the building was used for a long time as a gun powder store and it was not pulled down. Fortunately it was not blown up. It was restored on several occasions, recently in 1963.

The turbe was built in 1591. The structure on an octagonal groundplan is covered by a *spherical segment cupola* 6 m in diameter.

SPOTS OF INTEREST IN THE MECSEK

We cannot speak about Pécs without mentioning the Mecsek. In fact the town itself merges with the Mecsek side and gradually climbs upward. The regrettable consequence of this process is that the green slopes behind the town are becoming gray with modern buildings, and the natural park of Pécs and "lung of the town" is continuously retreating.

In the 18th century, vineyards covered the downs. Later, building work started on the northern side of the walls, along former Petrezselyem (Parsley) street (today: Aradi vértanúk útja) and Kálvária (today: Vak Bottyán) utca. The nearest hill to the town is the K á l v á r i a. The first *stations* and the *crosses* as well as the baroque *gateway* were erected already in the 18th century. The present cast iron reliefs of the stations replaced the old reliefs in the second half of the 19th century. As a donation from the weaver, József Ábel, the cupola covered neo-classic *church,* on a circular ground plan, and with a small turret, was built in 1814.

Hunyadi János út, which climbs up the mountain, is crossed by an artificially built east-west road before reaching the Mecsek. This was called Magaslati út (Height road), at present—to the west—it is S u r á - n y i M i k l ó s and towards the Tettye—to the east— K a l i n y i n ú t. Those who designed the street hoped to have set up a favourite pedestrian precinct of the town. Therefore, they wanted to leave the southern side free and the *benches* along the road were turned towards the town, so that the strollers when resting should be able to admire the wonderful panorama. However, modern architecture deprived the strollers of this panorama. Ultra modern oversized houses were constructed alongside the first *villas,* which were built on the northern side with great care. Only the small square and behind it, the *Paulite Church* remained from the original idea. The church was built in 1938 designed by Károly Weichinger. The statue of the *Virgin Mary* made from white glazed pyrogranite by András Sinkó, was unveiled in 1948, beside the modern natural stone church. From the south, the church can be approached on broad *steps*. The porcelain faience *Symbol statue* by Victor Vasarely is displayed in the small park in front of the steps.

H u n y a d i J á n o s ú t, which leads to the north alongside the Paulite church, goes up to the Resort Hotel with sharp bends at the Mecsek Gate.

82 A   **Liberation Monument** (Hunyadi János út). It was erected in 1975, on the 30th anniversary of Hungary's liberation, as a result of social cohesion. It can be seen from almost every point of the town, as it was built on an extremely emphasized place of the Mecsek side. Its white concrete architecture was designed by György Jánossy, and the *statue* from welded bronze is the work of Makrisz Agamemnon, a Hungarian sculptor of Greek background. The dynamic statue is of symbolic force: it symbolizes Nike, the Greek goddess of victory. A square was also built around the memorial, suitable for rallies, from where an unparalleled panorama opens over the town.

83 A   **SZOT (Trade Unio) Holiday Resort** (Hunyadi János út). The former impressive Kikelet Hotel was built in 1935, based on the design of László Lauber. The building contractor was the excellent builder, Andor Márovits (Marsay) of Pécs. His most significant buildings in Pécs are the Paulite Church, the Law Faculty of the University, the Forbáth House in Felsőmalom utca, and Mór College.

84 A   **French Memorial** (near to the SZOT Resort on the road leading to the Fenyves Hotel). It was erected in 1908. The French eagle—resting on the multistepped polarised truncated pyramid, on a natural stone base—symbolizes the eternal rest of French soldiers who were captured in the French war (1808) and died at Pécs. The inscription on the memorial indicates this: "In memory of the soldiers of the glorious Grand Army on the centenary of their death—in gallant sympathy from their Hungarian friends, 1908."

The road leading along the SZOT Resort winds at the Pécs Zoo and forks in two directions. The road leading to the east (to the right) takes the traffic to *Dömör-kapu* (Guesthouse, Cultural Park of Pécs) and to the *Television Tower* (Television espresso bar, Misina Restaurant) situated on the Misina peak.

POINTS WORTH NOTING

GENERAL INFORMATION

Pécs has 172,000 *inhabitants*. Its *highest points*: Misina-csúcs 534 m, Lapis 535 m, Tubes 612 m, and Jakab-hegy 602 m.

Post: Pécs No. 1 Post Office: Jókai u. 10. Open: from Monday to Friday 08.00—20.00, Saturday 08.00—14.00, Sunday 08.00—12.00. No. 2 Post Office: at the main railway station, open: from Monday to Thursday 08.00—16.00, Friday 08.00—17.00. 15 more post offices operate on various points of the town.

TRANSPORT

MÁV

Several scheduled lines operate between Budapest—Pécs—Budapest every day. On the Mecsek and Baranya express trains, seat reservation is necessary. There is a direct link between Nagykanizsa—Szombathely, Mohács, Bátaszék—Baja—Szeged and Beli Monastir (Yugoslavia), as well as to Lake Balaton on the route: Pécs—Kaposvár—Fonyód—Siófok, and to Keszthely and Tapolca.

Volán

Scheduled long-distance coaches travel to Pécs—Szekszárd—Budapest, Kaposvár, Hévíz, Baja—Szeged, Baja—Kecskemét and Veszprém, to the towns and villages of the county, and to Osijek in Yugoslavia. *Information:* available by telephone — 15-665. A new bus terminal was opened in 1982 between Szalai András and Rózsa Ferenc streets.

Roads

Budapest—Pécs 197 km, Pécs—Sásd—Boglárlelle 131 km, Pécs—Mohács—Bátaszék—Baja—Szeged 190 km, Pécs—Osijek 96 km and Pécs—Barcs—Virovitica—Bjelovar—Zagreb 230 km.

Local public transport

Main lines: bus No. 10, 20 and 40 go to Újmecsekalja (the latter calls at the railway station). Bus No. 30 runs from the railway station via Széchenyi tér to the Teachers' Training College of the Janus Pannonius University, No. 33 between Kossuth tér and Tettye, No. 34 to Dömör-kapu and No. 35 to the Misina (TV Tower). Lvov suburb can be reached by No. 16, 47 and 39.

Detailed information: available on the local time tables.

Taxi

Taxi stands are located in various points of the town (Széchenyi tér, railway station, Zsolnay factory, and at the Olimpia Restaurant at Újmecsekalja, etc.) Tel.: 10-333, 10-532.

FOR MOTORISTS

Repairs

AFIT No. 14/V, Szigeti út 131. Tel.: 24-499. Guaranteed and emergency repairs, preparation for technical tests and testing, diagnostics, consumption checks and adjustments, and breakdown service.

VILLGÉP, Diósi út 49. Tel.: 14-479, 14-496. Repairs and servicing of all types of cars, and chassis treatment.

SHELL service and petrol station, Pécsváradi u. 27.

Tel.: 13-063. Maintenance, service, emergency repairs and diagnostics.

Tyres: Bajcsy-Zsilinszky u. 12. Tel.: 19-875.

Petrol

Day-and-night service at the ÁFOR—BP petrol stations at Fürst Sándor út, at Hajnóczy utca (Újmecsekalja) and on road No. 6 at the Kővágószőlős fork, as well as SHELL stations on road No. 6 and at Bolgár Néphadsereg u. 104/a. Petrol stations with shorter opening hours are at Steinmetz kapitány tér and Kandó Kálmán utca.

ACCOMMODATION

Hotels

Pannónia ***, Rákóczi út 3. Tel.: 13-322. Telex: 12-469, 108 double rooms, with bath (extra bed available in 15) five suites.

Nádor **, Széchenyi tér 15. Tel.: 11-477. Telex: 12-200, 31 double rooms, with bath (extra bed available), one suite, 27 double rooms with extra bed without bath. Facilities (in addition to the basic amenities): individual guiding with taperecorder and map in 4 languages, free entrance to the Hullám Bath and entrance to the museums. Television and radio sets in most rooms.

Hunyor **, (Jurisics Miklós utca, next to the Szőlőskert Restaurant). Managed by Mecsektourist. 51 double rooms with bath, and terrace to the south (some with extra bed), in-house telephone, two suites (two rooms with 2+1 beds), in-house telephone. Banqueting hall for 80, television lounge for 50. Cark park in front of the building for 28 cars and 2 coaches. The hotel is connected with the neighbouring Szőlőskert (Vineyard) Restaurant by a promenade and closed corridor.

Fenyves, Szőlő u. 64. Tel.: 15-996.

Dömörkapu, Gyükés dűlő 1. Tel.: 15-987. At the terminal of bus No. 34 in the Mecsek.

Rest house

Kastély Fogadó, managed by the Pécs State Farm, alongside road No. 57, between Pécs and Mohács, at Üszögpuszta, in an 18th century baroque castle. One suite, two rooms with bath, two mansard rooms with bath, five mansard rooms with public bath, and three wooden chalets with double room and extra beds, heating, warm water shower. Reservations through the IBUSZ Office at Pécs, or Pécsi Állami Gazdaság, Üszögpuszta, POB 168, 7601 Pécs.

Paying guest service

Single and double rooms, with available extra bed, in private homes in the town or in the resort area of the Mecsek Park and forest, can be booked through the Mecsektourist travel agency in Pécs, Széchenyi tér 1. Tel.: 14-866. Telex: 12-238, or can be reserved through any travel agency and IBUSZ Office in Hungary.

Camping

Mecseki Mandulás Camping site. Tel.: 15-981. Open between April 15 and October 15. There is a *rest house* on the camp site with a double room and wash basin.

Holiday chalets with three bedded rooms and shower. There are also second and third class chalets with two and four beds. Holiday-makers with their own tent or caravan can be accommodated, electric points, car wash facilities, cooking, washing and shower facilities provided.

MEALS

Restaurants, coffee and drinks

Pannónia Restaurant, first class, with music, seating for 260, banqueting hall for 100, and summer terrace for 130. Drink bar, and espresso. Rákóczi u. 3. Tel.: 13-322.

Nádor Restaurant, first class, with music, seating for 250, banqueting halls for 40 and 80 guests, Nádor Kávéház (Coffee-house) seats 110.

Nádor Beerhall, second class, seating for 90, Széchenyi tér 15.

Minaret Restaurant, second class, seating for 110, banqueting hall for 30, garden barbecue for 110+30. Sallai u. 35. Tel.: 13-322.

Eszék Restaurant, in Bajcsy-Zsilinszky utca, open every day (opened in 1981).

Kazinczy Restaurant, Kazinczy u. 6.

Finom Falatok Boltja bistro, Kossuth L. u. 1.

Terasz Presszó (Terrace espresso) on Színház tér is open during the summer.

Építők (Builders) *Restaurant,* Szántó-Kovács János u. 1.

Ságvári Restaurant, Hajnóczi u. 41. Újmecsekalja.

Restaurants of the Baranya County Catering Company: Fenyves, Dömörkapu—in the hotels, Susogó and Tettye in the Mecsek, the Misina Restaurant in the TV Tower, the Aranykacsa, Hullám, Sopianae, Borostyán and Szliven in the inner-city, and the Olimpia at Újmecsekalja.

Wild game delicacies at the Vadásztanya at the corner of Ürögi and Jakab-hegyi street, and *fish dishes* at the Halétterem of the Bikali State Farm at the corner of Szabadság utca and József Attila út.

Konzum Restaurant, second class, on the corner of Kossuth tér and Bem utca. A self-service restaurant open from 06.30—20.30 with hot and cold dishes, and drinks. A traditional restaurant open from Tuesday to Friday 17.00—23.00, and Saturday and Sunday from 11.00 with excellent dishes, drinks and music.

Tv-körpresszó in the Television Tower on the Misina peak in the Mecsek. Tel.: 12-044. Open in the high-season 09.30—20.30, in the off-season 09.30—19.00.

Diána Restaurant in the Lvov garden city.

Espressos

Mecsek Cukrászda (cake shop), first class, with music. Széchenyi tér 15.

In various parts of the town: Éva, Jókai, Kuba, Művész, Misina, Kolumbia and Napsugár, etc., espressos.

Garden restaurants

The Rózsakert, Olimpia, Fenyves, Tettye, Susogó, Aranykacsa, Mecsek, Dömörkapu and Szőlőskert restaurants have gardens.

Wine tasting

István pince (Stephen cellar), Kazinczy u. 2, and in front of Rózsakert, the Borkóstoló (Wine tasting) in Janus Pannonius utca.

Barbakán Bár (Barbican bar), Landler Jenő u. 18. Tel.: 24-930. Opened in the old town wall in 1981. Managed by the Pannónia Áfész, it is open from 09.00—19.00, and the bar from 19.00—02.00.

Barlang Borozó (Cave wine bar), Munkácsy Mihály utca.

Bistros and shops

Tejbisztró (Milk bar) in Jókai tér and the *Baranya* in Hal tér. At Újmecsekalja along road No. 6, the No. 100 *SM food store* in the Lvov suburb and *ABC supermarkets* in the southern new district.

A *grocery store and snack bar* are open to tourists from 07.00—19.00 opposite the SZOT Holiday Resort.

SPECIALLY FOR TOURISTS

Travel agencies

Mecsektourist Travel Agency Pécs Office. Széchenyi tér 1. Tel.: 14-866. Telex: 12-238. Information, MÁV and MALÉV ticket reservations, sale of socialist countries' currencies, exchange of currency, sale of Dinars to travellers to Yugoslavia, group travel in Hungary and abroad, excursions, organisation of functions, visits to displays and art monuments (e.g. the Cathedral, mosque of Hassan Jakovali, synagogue, and turbe of Baba Idris, etc.). Guides. Sale of tourist publications. From spring until autumn open on Sunday from 09.00—12.00, and on week days (with the exception of Monday) extended office hours.

Mecsek Tourist Central Office. Széchenyi tér 9. Tel.: 13-300. Telex: 12-213. Reservation of accommodation for the entire county. Letters: POB 129, 7601 Pécs.

IBUSZ Travel Agency. Széchenyi tér 8. (Letters: POB 81, 7601 Pécs). Trips abroad, visa, group tours in Hungary, accommodation, transport tickets, individual trips abroad (Tel.: 12-148), recuperational holidays and passports (Tel.: 12-169). Currency exhange (Tel.: 12-176). Room reservation for the tourist hostel at Szilágypuszta and in the Kastély Fogadó (Üszögpuszta). The latter offers riding programmes and excellent cuisine for its guests.

Baranya County Office of the Express Youth and Students' Travel Bureau. Bajcsy-Zsilinszky u. 6, 7622 Pécs. Tel.: 12-793. Telex: 12-312. Group and individual travel in Hungary and abroad, organisation of functions and programmes, accommodation (in the summer also in students' hostels), guides, exchange of currency and sale, coach rental, transport tickets in Hungary and abroad, and sale of international youth cards.

Cooptourist Travel Agency. Kossuth Lajos u. 33. Tel.: 13-407. Group tours in Hungary and abroad, holidays, and currency exchange.

Volán Travel Agency. Déryné u. 1. Tel.: 11-326. Telex: 12-214. Group tours in Hungary and abroad, excursions, car rental, and reservation of coach tickets.

Hungarian Camping and Caravanning Club Bara-

nya County Organisation. Széchenyi tér 9. Tel.: 11-622. Membership admission. International camping card. Information. Open: Tuesday and Thursday 09.00— 12.00 and 14.00—18.00.

Guides

Mecsektourist, IBUSZ and Express provide guides for sightseeing, county round-trips, and conducted tours in Hungary and abroad.

Currency exchange

In the Mecsektourist Travel Office, Széchenyi tér 1.; IBUSZ Office, Széchenyi tér 8.; Cooptourist, Kossuth Lajos u. 33.; Express, Bajcsy-Zsilinszky u. 6.; and the OTP, Kossuth Lajos u. 11.

ENTERTAINMENT

Cinemas

Kossuth, Perczel u. 22. Tel.: 13-442. Six performances daily, continuous from 10.00.

Park, Felsőmalom u. 23. Tel.: 11-222. Three performances daily.

Park-kert, Felsőmalom u. 23. One open-air evening performance daily between May 15 and September 15.

Petőfi, Doktor Sándor u. 19. Tel.: 12-211. Three performances daily.

Theatre

Pécs National Theatre, Színház tér. Tel.: 11-965. Dramas, operas, operettas, ballet performances, and plays for children from October to June in the National and Chamber Theatres, generally at 19.00 on workdays and at 15.00 and 19.00 on holidays. Closed on Tuesday.

Bóbita Puppet Theatre, Déryné u. 18. Performances on Sunday morning at 10.00 and on Saturday at 10.00 and 15.00.

"Pécsi Műsor"

A monthly providing information on the programmes of the cultural centres, the Pécs filial of the National Philharmonia, the ORI National Concert Bureau, the Youth House and sports hall. It also publishes the detailed programme schedule of the cinemas, theatres and other events.

Bathing

Balokány Bath. Zsolnay V. u. 46. Open between June and August. *Hullám Bath.* József Attila u. 10. Open from May until the end of August. Between September and April, the Sports and Training Pool under the Graboplast tent is open.

Nagy Lajos Bath (in the courtyard of the Grammar School) open from June—August.

Tub Baths. Rákóczi út 58. Various balneological facilities available (mud bath and traction bath, etc.).

Mecsek cultural park

Fun Fair (in the Mecsek at Dömörkapu). Open: from April until the end of October, daily from 10.00 until dusk. Closed on Monday. Tel.: 12-788.

Zoo (in the Mecsek, at the bus stop after the SZOT Holiday Resort). Open: all the year round, daily from 09.00—17.00.

Pioneer Railway between the Zoo and the Fun Fair, on Sundays and holidays, between 09.00—17.00, every 15 minutes.

Kreszpark (Highway code training ground) at Újmecsekalja. Open: April—October, daily from 08.00—17.00. Closed on Monday. Tel.: 12-100.

Planetarium

Hungary's first small planetarium operates on the Mecsek side, at Szőlő u. 65/4 (Tel.: 15-772) in the Natural Scientific Studio of the Society for the Dissemination of Scientific Knowledge. The star studded sky is projected onto the interior of the cupola, onto this artificial sky, with optical medium type instruments of the Zeiss Works. Groups can be announced by telephone, daily from 09.00—17.00. For interested individuals, lectures are delivered every Saturday and Sunday at 16.30.

Artificial ice rink

Veress Endre u. 4. Tel.: 24-923. Open from mid-October until mid-March, daily 09.00—12.00, 14.00—16.00, and 17.00—19.00. Closed on Monday.

Tennis

At the above mentioned address, three synthetic covered courts are available from May to September. Open from 06.00—12.00 and 14.00—20.00. Bookings and reservations in the Mecsektourist offices.

Riding

The riding school, race and training course of the Pécs State Farm at Üszögpuszta is also suitable for international races. Thirty Hungarian halfbreds, Lippizans and English thoroughbreds are available in the stables. The specialists of the riding school help to select the suitable horses and accompany guests on pony trekking. Facilities: riding on lunge, class riding in the riding school, pony trekking and two-in-hand carriage driving. Riding courses for children. Detailed information from the IBUSZ Office (Széchenyi tér 7. Tel.: 12-143) and the Pécs State Farm (Üszögpuszta).

133

Pintér garden

Managed by the South Transdanubian Directorate of the National Office for the Protection of the Environment and Nature. (Tettye tér 9., Pécs. Tel.: 24-249). The Garden can be visited between April 1—October 31. The dendrological garden developed since the turn of the century, was owned by János Pintér. In 1976 it was declared a nature reservation of national significance. Its area covers about two hectares. There are roughly 240 different species of trees and bushes in the garden. Its rareties are: the Arizona cypress, the Japanese white pine, the Nevada cembra pine, many rare plants of the Mecsek mountain and other Mediterranean plants. The permanent exhibition of the *Villány Statue Park* is a noteworthy spectacle.

Museums, Exhibitions

Archeological Exhibition. The history of Baranya from ancient times to the Árpád era. Széchenyi tér 12. Open: 10.00—18.00. Closed on Monday. Visitors can become acquainted with the relics of ancient times—found in Baranya County—including the *Madonna of Zengővárkony* of cultic purpose, then the life of the Province of Pannonia of the Roman Empire, and the preserved objects of the ethnic groups, which alternated during the Migration.

Vasarely Museum. Káptalan u. 3. Open: 10.00—18.00. Closed on Monday. The Museum was opened in 1976 and introduces the art of Victor Vasarely (originally Győző Vásárhelyi of Pécs), the initiator of "op art". In addition to his works, the museum also houses artifacts by his wife, Claire Vasarely. The graphic works of his son, Jean-Pierre Yvaral, are also on display in the Museum.

Zsolnay Ceramic Exhibition. Káptalan u. 2. Open: 10.00—18.00. Closed on Monday. The artistic productions of the Factory, ranging from the 1870s up to the present time, are on display. The most significant characteristics of the local style, technical methods,

134

types of glaze and the best yield of the different artists are illustrated.

Renaissance display of stones. Káptalan u. 2. Open: May 1—October 31 on Saturday and Sunday between 10.00—18.00. Many relics survived from the renaissance, an artistically important period in the development of Pécs, which flourished in the Middle Ages. A well supplemented and interpreted collection of the stone material, extant from those times, is displayed in the museum.

Roman Sepulchre Chapel. Geisler Eta u. 14. Open: May 1—October 31, daily between 10.00—13.00 and 15.00—18.00. Closed on Monday. According to the findings, the building dates back to about 320 A. D. It was a large burial vault in which the graves of three adults and one child were found.

Roman sepulchres. Geisler Eta u. 8. Open: May 1—October 31, daily between 10.00—13.00 and 15.00—18.00. Closed on Monday. Several graves can be seen in the small museum room, each on its original site. The findings from the graves are also on display.

Hassan Jakovali Museum. Rákóczi u. 2. Open: 10.00—18.00. Closed on Wednesday. The exhibition in the mosque of Pasha Hassan Jakovali, one of the most intact buildings from the period of the Turkish occupation, and in the entrance hall to the mosque—illustrates the Turkish era in Pécs and Baranya with historic and cultural historic documents. Its unique feature in that with the help of the gift by the Turkish government, the interior of a 16th century Turkish mosque was reconstructed in the djami.

Baranya népe. Rákóczi u. 15. Open: 10.00—13.00 and 15.00—18.00. Closed on Monday. The rich enthic and folklore material of the Hungarian population of Baranya County, of its large Serb and Croatian ethnic groups and German minority—is exhibited.

Modern Hungarian Gallery. Szabadság u. 2. Open: 10.00—18.00. Closed on Monday. A rich and broad scale display of Hungarian fine arts, ranging from the turn of the century to the present time.

Uitz Museum. Káptalan u. 4. Open: 10.00—13.00 and 15.00—18.00. Closed on Monday. The art of Béla Uitz, an eminent representative of Hungarian revolutionary fine art from the beginning of the century, is illustrated in the premises of the baroque palace, reconstructed from an originally Gothic building. The exhibition illustrates the outstanding periods of his oeuvre: the excellent recruiting poster "Forward Red soldiers!" from the time of the 1919 Hungarian Republic of Councils and his series of etchings "General Ludd" depicting the English weavers' revolution, was made in 1923 in Vienna. From the years of his Moscow emigration, fresco designs and portraits provide a good selection.

Permanent exhibition of Ferenc Martyn's drawings.
Káptalan u. 6. Open: 10.00—14.00. Closed on Monday.

Csontváry Museum. Janus Pannonius u. 11. Open: 10.00—18.00. Closed on Monday. The Museum was opened in 1973, on the 120th anniversary of the birth of Tivadar Csontváry Kosztka. The main works of this eminent Hungarian painter and the drawings of his early period are on display. The visionary and symbolic content of Csontváry's art made him an early forerunner of expressionism and surrealistic trends. "Baalbek" of extremely large dimensions is a fascinating work, where monumentality and the richness of details, symbolic interpretation and the post-impressionist colour intensification are of equal significance. Csontváry painted with a passionate dedication and consciousness, withdrawn, nevertheless, longing for the nourishing community. The keen interest in his works justifies the appreciation of his greatness.

The exhibition emphasizes the leading artists and main directions of the Hungarian avant garde, the group of Eight, and the Activists, the abstract trends from the first half of this century, and the varied genres of the latest period, as well as the art of innovatory aspirations. A group of the founding collection is displayed in a separate cabinet, the statues by Erzsébet Forgács Hann. The statues by Amerigo Tot (originally Imre Tóth) represent a separate unit, which the artist of Hungarian origin, but living in Rome, donated to the Museum in 1978.

In the autumn of 1982, the Museum was enriched with further significant artistic creations: 227 valuable paintings, statues and graphics from the private collection of Academician Dr. Gábor Ubrizsy, came to Pécs. Most of the exhibits are from the 20th century, but some paintings of maestroes from the past century are also included.

Mecsek and its region. Rákóczi út 64. Open: Tuesday and Friday from 15.00—18.00, on Saturday and Sunday from 10.00—13.00, and from 15.00—18.00. Closed on Monday. Baranya bordered by the Mecsek mountain, which is considered the northernmost foothills of the Mediterranean region,—in addition to the flora, fauna and insects to be found also in other places of the country—is the land of many rareties. The exhibition illustrates the minerals and living world of this region.

Mining Museum. Déryné u. 9. Open: from 09.00—17.00. Closed on Monday. Technical and management historical exhibition of Mecsek coal and ore mining, as well as the working class movement exhibition—pay homage to work and to the miners.

The world of stones. Káptalan u. 3. Open: 09.00—17.00. Closed on Monday. The underground museum in a purposefully arranged part of the old cellar system, which is so characteristic of the town, imitating the miners' milieu, introduces the world of minerals in Hungary.

Cathedral. István tér. Open: 09.00—13.00 and 14.00—18.00. On Sunday and on religious holidays it can be visited between 12.30—17.00. Professional guides for groups of adults and children.

Mosque of Pasha Kassim Gazi (today: Inner-city Church). Széchenyi tér. Open all day. On Sundays and religious holidays it can be visited from 12.30.

Turbe of Baba Idris. Nyár u. 8. Open: from April 1—October 31. Closed on Monday. Guided tours for organised groups.

Synagogue. Eastern side of Kossuth tér. Open: Monday—Thursday and on Sunday 09.00—13.00 and 14.00—17.30. On Friday between 09.00—13.00 and 14.00—16.00. Closed on Wednesday. From April 15—October 15 the synagogue is open according to the above. It can be visited at other times by prior appointment with Mecsektourist. A synagogue in a romantic style (of neologian rite) with two galleries above each other in its interior.

Bath of Pasha Memi. In front of the buildings. Sallai u. 33 and 35. Open: April—October between 09.00—13.00 and 14.00—18.00. It was one of the three Turkish baths, which operated in Pécs. The ornamental running fountain in the centre of its foyer is a reconstruction, based on the found fragments.

Pécs Gallery. Széchenyi köz. Every month a different fine art exhibition is held in the Gallery (e.g. the Small Plastic Biennale and the National Ceramics Biennale, etc.). Open: between 10.00—18.00. Closed on Tuesday. Details about the current exhibitions are given in the monthly "Pécsi Műsor".

OTHER POINTS OF INTEREST

During a stroll through Pécs, one should visit the *episcopal garden* beside the Cathedral, the *Barbican,* the *Liberation Monument* on the Mecsek side, the *forest sports grounds* in the Éger valley, the *Tettye* and so on. During a visit to the Mecsek, one must not miss the 198 m high *Television Tower* on the Misina peak (534 m), which was built next to the former Kiss József look-out tower. A circular espresso bar offers refreshments in the tower at a height of 98 m, and above it a wonderful view opens onto the region from the circular balcony.

SHOPPING

One of the busiest shopping centres of Pécs is the *Konzum Áruház* (Department store) at Kossuth tér in the centre of the town, with a large variety of goods in its food store, clothing and miscellaneous departments. Snack bar, lift, escalators and car park ensure comfortable and easy shopping facilities.

The *Centrum Áruház* is also in the centre, on the corner of Kossuth Lajos utca and Széchenyi tér. It is open from 08.30—19.00, on Thursday from 08.00—20.00 and on Saturday 08.30—14.00.

Terlyszter Mintabolt (Textiles). Jókai tér 2.

Centrum Divatbolt (Fashion clothing). Kossuth Lajos u. 15.

Gloves and Leatherware. Sallai u. 8.

Mecsektourist souvenir shop. At the foot of the Television Tower. Tourist publications, souvenirs and postcards, etc.